The Language-Experience Approach to Reading

A Handbook for Teachers

The Language-Experience Approach to Reading

A Handbook for Teachers

Denise D. Nessel

Margaret B. Jones

 **Teachers College
Columbia University
New York & London 1981**

Published by Teachers College Press, 1234 Amsterdam Avenue,
New York, N.Y. 10027

Library of Congress Cataloging in Publication Data

Nessel, Denise D   1943-
   The language-experience approach to
reading.

   Includes bibliographical references and index.
   1. Reading (Primary)—Language experience approach.
2. First grade (Education) I. Jones, Margaret B.,
1928- joint author. II. Title.
LB1525.34.N47   372.4'14   80-27822
ISBN 0-8077-2596-X (pbk.)
ISBN 0-8077-2652-4 (cloth)

Manufactured in the United States of America

92   91   90   89   88   87   4   5   6   7   8   9   10

To
Dorothy N. Brosius
and
Monica F. Nessel

Contents

Tables

Acknowledgments

To Dr. Russell G. Stauffer we extend our appreciation for teaching us about the language-experience approach. We learned much from him that is reflected in this book: our basic philosophy of reading instruction and insights into beginning reading. We would also like to acknowledge Dr. Marian Stauffer for her skill in working with teachers and her willingness to share her ideas. She, too, has contributed to our thinking.

Special thanks go to Joan Balascio Phillips, a teacher who used our ideas and gave us many in return which we have shared here; to Peggy Shultz, a reading specialist who helped develop and test some assessment strategies; and to Dr. John J. Pikulski, who has offered us continued support and encouragement.

Finally, we thank the teachers of Avon Grove School District (West Grove, Pennsylvania), West Chester Area School District (West Chester, Pennsylvania), the Dorchester County Schools (Dorchester County, Maryland), and the Charles County Schools (Charles County, Maryland), who worked with us to make the language-experience approach a success in many classrooms.

The Language-Experience Approach to Reading

A Handbook for Teachers

Chapter I

Introduction

The language-experience approach (LEA) is a means of teaching students to read by capitalizing on their interests, experiences, and oral language facility. Students dictate stories and accounts based on their experiences; these materials are then used as the basis of the reading program. The procedure is based on two assumptions: that interests and life experiences are of great personal value and are highly meaningful to students; and that learning to read is easiest and most enjoyable when reading materials match the language patterns and speaking vocabularies of the readers. LEA can be used with beginning readers of all ages; it is useful as a kindergarten or first-grade program, as a supplement to upper-grade language arts and content-area instruction, and as a tutorial procedure for severely disabled readers. In fact, good teachers at all levels often use many of the basic principles of LEA in their instructional programs.

Several texts give detailed discussions of the rationale of language-experience and also present general explanations of instructional strategies used in an LEA program.* On the other hand, some publications offer a carefully structured sequence of language-experience activities that may not be appropriate in all classrooms.** Few resources give specific, practical ideas for lessons and reinforcement activities and also enable teachers to use their own ideas in choosing topics for dictation, designing creative activities, and in other ways tailoring the reading program to the needs of a specific group.

Over a period of several years we have helped classroom teachers and reading clinicians implement the language-experience approach in their classes. Repeatedly we have seen the need for a useful handbook that outlines specific LEA procedures and offers more than is currently available in the way of suggested activities for a total program. We have written this handbook to offer practical help to teachers who want to design their own creative language-experience programs. The suggestions in this book are based on experiences in many classrooms. In fact, many of the specific teaching activities are borrowed directly from creative teachers who have expanded on our ideas and suggestions.

We have emphasized applications in first-grade classrooms because it is at this level that LEA is most widely and most often used. We also suggest several variations on basic procedures in the hope that our readers will go beyond our suggestions in using language-experience wherever it seems applicable.

We see language-experience in first grade as an approach that will give children both beginning reading skills and positive attitudes toward the world of books and reading. We describe ways of using LEA in lieu of the readiness and preprimer components of a basal series; most children using the program we outline will move into a regular primer or first reader sometime in the first-grade year. While we cannot argue that there is greater measurable achievement at the end of first grade when LEA is used in this way, we do believe that children's willingness to read, their positive feelings about school, and their interest in books all are greater when they are taught in an LEA program than when they are taught using only a traditional basal reader series.

A principal we know made the same subjective judgment of the language-experience program in his school. He pointed out that there was little difference in end-of-first-grade reading achievement between children in the LEA classrooms and children in the traditional basal classrooms. He further observed that youngsters in the total basal program were "schoolwise" when taking standardized tests and when entering second grade, where they encountered myriad texts and worksheets. However, he added ruefully that this schoolwise attitude was developed at a price. Unlike the LEA children, who had experienced only pleasure and success with reading, these children had learned that reading could be hard and that they could fail. Also unlike the LEA children, who had read about topics ranging from applesauce to sharks, those in a total basal program had had their formal reading instruction limited to the content of the basal materials.

This handbook will be most useful to teachers and reading specialists who have had some teaching experience and who are familiar with most of the general principles of the language-experience approach. Although most of the suggestions are described with first graders in mind, the sample lessons and activities can be adapted to classrooms and tutorial situations at any level. We have attempted to build a good amount of flexibility into the guidelines we recommend so that teachers will use their own judgment about which ideas are most suitable for the children in their classes. Using LEA as we suggest will not be easy. Careful thought, good planning, and a sensitive, creative approach to students are all needed to put these ideas into practice. But to the teacher who wants to learn about children and reading and is eager to design a unique program, we think we have something to say.

---

*Mary Ann Hall, *Teaching Reading as a Language Experience* (Columbus, Ohio: Charles Merrill, 1976).

Russell G. Stauffer, *The Language-Experience Approach to the Teaching of Reading* (New York: Harper & Row, 1970).

J. Veatch, F. Sawicki, G. Elliott, E. Barnette, and J. Blakey, *Key Words to Reading: The Language-Experience Approach Begins* (Columbus, Ohio: Charles Merrill, 1973).

**R. Van Allen, *Language Experiences in Reading* (Chicago: Encyclopaedia Britannica Press, 1969).

Chapter II

Group-Dictated Stories: First Steps

In this chapter we will present the basic procedures used in the initial stages of a language-experience program—the methods used to obtain dictated stories and to prepare the instructional materials for skill development that are an outgrowth of those stories. There are five steps in the cycle:

1. Preparing for dictation
2. Taking dictation
3. Reading the story
4. Conducting immediate follow-up activities
5. Developing basic skills

The first four steps are best accomplished in one session. The fifth step ordinarily requires two to four sessions to complete. Thus, if one session is planned per day, these five basic steps can be accomplished in approximately one week. At the end of this time the cycle is repeated; i.e., a new dictated story is obtained and the same steps used to develop reading skills further. Approximately one dictated story a week is obtained from each group that is using the program. Some groups will require a day or two more to complete the basic procedures; some will require slightly less time before moving on to another experience story.

PREPARING FOR DICTATION

The first step in the process of obtaining a dictated experience story is an oral language activity, most often a group discussion of an object or event. The quality of discussion and the exchange of ideas preceding dictation have a significant effect on the quality of the experience story. The teacher's objectives during this time should be to

1. Encourage careful observation of the stimulus
2. Elicit and extend oral language relating to the children's thoughts and observations
3. Encourage listening to and responding to classmates' observations

This predictation activity provides a good opportunity to build oral language skills and to ensure that reading instruction proceeds as part of a total language arts program. It is a very important step in the process and should be planned and conducted with care.

The three major objectives of the oral language activity will be met most effectively if teachers ask questions as well as give information. Questions should be open ended and should encourage the expression of complete thoughts as much as possible. For instance, if a group is examining a hamster, questions like these would be appropriate:

What is the hamster doing now?
What do you notice about his fur?
How does the hamster feel when you touch him?
What do you like best about the hamster?

Of course the teacher can enter into the discussion with comments and observations. The teacher's statements can extend children's perceptions and may also introduce additional vocabulary for children to incorporate into their own statements. The following exchange illustrates how teacher comments can serve this purpose. The group is examining a bowl of goldfish.

T: What do you notice about the fish?
Jay: They're all swimming around at the top.
Marcia: Look at where the wings move by his eyes.
T: Yes, they do look like wings. Does anyone know what they are called? (No response from the group.) Those are the fish's gills. The gills help him breathe.
Jay: He must be breathing fast. His gills are really moving.

This is not to suggest that the teacher must introduce relevant vocabulary. Discussion should flow naturally, with the teacher participating as one member of the group, not as the dominant member. Sometimes children will pick up new words and ideas introduced by the teacher; sometimes the teacher will not add new vocabulary to the general discussion. Most important is that the teacher encourage pupil talk rather than structuring the session around teacher talk.

Many objects, experiences, and ideas can provide stimuli for oral language and lead to good dictated stories. Here are some stimuli we have used or seen used that have resulted in excellent discussions and stories:

hamsters	turtles	kittens
rabbits	chameleons	guinea pigs
goldfish	puppies	snakes

These are all, of course, live stimuli that move around, make noise, and do interesting things like eat, sneeze, and play, all of which can be noted, described, and discussed. Such live stimuli usually bring about much oral language and provide the foundation for a meaningful dictating experience.

There is no need, however, to go to great expense in selecting a stimulus. We once worked with the first-grade teachers in a school that had just decided to implement the language-experience approach. After we suggested some stimuli that could be used for dictated stories, one teacher spent most of a weekend shopping for a white rabbit. Of course the children were enchanted with the rabbit, but the discussion was no better than one conducted in the room down the hall by a teacher who brought in a house plant and engaged the children in a lively talk about leaves, stems, soil, and water. The novelty of a stimulus is less important than the observations and discussion resulting from the experience. For instance, we recall one occasion when one of us simply said to a group, "I notice you are all wearing different kinds of shoes today. Let's look at our shoes and see what we can learn." The discussion was filled with good observations of similarities and differences in the shoes. Classification of colors, styles, and purposes of shoes resulted. One boy even coined the term *undershoes* to describe his socks.

With these ideas in mind we can suggest some other types of stimuli that we have also found work quite well in engaging children's attention, interest, and oral language. These include:

a musical instrument	the clock in the room
house plants or terrariums	money
a thermometer (with	photographs of classroom
glasses of hot and cold	activities
water for moving the	illustrations from
mercury)	magazines

the school P.A. system as
  seen from the office
a visit to a farm, hospital
  or other interesting
  place
holiday preparations or
  reflections
a toy
a cooking lesson
school sports events

the first snow storm
seasonal topics (such as a
  group's Halloween
  costumes)
a doll collection
shells
rocks
a filmstrip
a piece of leather
tools

Some stimuli may be inappropriate because the objects are too valuable or dangerous to entrust to eager small children. For instance, an unfortunate incident occurred when a teacher brought in a lovely collection of dried wild flowers and passed the album around for inspection. In their eagerness to see and feel, the children inadvertently damaged several of the flowers, to the regret of the teacher and children alike. Delicate Christmas ornaments, antique dolls, or collections of glass animals might all pose similar difficulties if used as stimuli. Another teacher was quite cautious when she brought in an asparagus cutter. Concerned for the children's safety, she wisely did not allow them to handle the sharp forked knife at all. Although no one was injured and nothing was damaged, the children were not able to examine the interesting tool thoroughly, and the experience and discussion were not as good as usual. Generally, fragile objects or potentially dangerous items are best left at home. The best stimuli are those that can be examined easily and safely and are sturdy enough to withstand handling.

Other cautions may also be necessary when choosing stimuli, in order to keep from interfering with parents' home regulations or beliefs. For instance, one parent was carefully planning the family's diet to avoid "junk" foods and other foods containing undesirable additives. That parent was very much concerned when the first grader came home telling about the great fun in reading class that day—the teacher had handed out brightly colored, candy-coated chocolate bits as a stimulus for a dictated story on different colors. Other parents may object to celebrating certain religious holidays or playing certain kinds of games and may be disturbed if dictated story stimuli conflict with their beliefs. These same kinds of conflicts also occur in classrooms where commercial materials are used, though the chance of displeasing parents is less with published programs since these are carefully screened to avoid most controversial material. Careful planning and good understanding of the community and of particular parents' values will help teachers avoid conflict with parents over the stimuli used for discussion in an LEA classroom.

Often the best stimuli are those things the children themselves bring to school—things relating to their hobbies, trips, and daily experiences. A hermit crab found at the shore, a baby rabbit discovered in the back yard, a model plane constructed at home are all good for sharing and use in dictations. Once children become involved in dictating stories based on their own favorite objects, their ideas for dictation topics will often far exceed those their teachers are able to think of. By noting what children bring to class to show and by listening to their talk about favorite interests and activities, the teacher will be able to glean many ideas of stimuli for dictated stories. One good example of a pupil-initiated topic involved a planorbis, a type of snail that keeps an aquarium clean by eating its way around the aquarium walls. A youngster brought a planorbis to class one day, a donation to the class aquarium from his aquarium at home. The children were fascinated with the snail and were especially interested in its long and difficult name. (The teacher learned something new that day, too, never having previously heard of a planorbis.) A delightful dictated story resulted from this experience.

THE PLANORBIS STORY

Luann said, "A planorbis always cleans
the side of the tank, but he doesn't do a
good job either." Kim said, "When the fish
eat, the planorbis cleans the side of the
tank for them." Mike said, "When they eat,
they move their jaws like we do."

If magazine pictures, books, or encyclopedia articles can be found relating to the topic of discussion, the teacher may want to have these available to show while the group is discussing the stimulus. A few moments spent showing the children printed information on the topic can enhance the discussion and also demonstrate that interesting information on all sorts of topics can be found in books.

As different stimuli are tried, brief notes should be made on the things used. It is easy to forget good ideas from one year to the next, so such a record is useful. The following sample illustrates the first part of such a record.

Date	Stimulus	Comments
9/5	Room aquarium	Had children feed fish; brought in fish books from library
9/13	Hamsters	Needed more time for discussion—hamsters active
9/20	Community helpers poster	Worked well; used police officer and firefighter pictures

A discussion of ten to fifteen minutes is probably adequate to stimulate ideas prior to dictation. Discussions may be longer, of course, depending on the children in the group, the daily schedule flexibility, or the group's response to a particular stimulus. A discussion should be long enough to stimulate ideas and allow good participation, yet brief enough to keep interest high.

TAKING DICTATION

A dictated account should be obtained from the group immediately after the discussion is completed, since it is important to capitalize on ideas that are fresh in the children's minds. Also, if the stimulus and discussion have captured the children's interest, the dictation and reading of the experience story can proceed while motivation is high.

The teacher should have the necessary materials ready and in place at this time. The following points concerning the mechanics of recording a story should help the procedure go smoothly:

1. Put the stimulus aside (out of sight if possible) so the children will be able to devote complete attention to the recording of their ideas.
2. Use a large, lined chart of oaktag or newsprint.
3. Have the chart attached to a good writing surface. Tape it to the chalkboard or a smooth wall or clip it on a large easel.
4. Use a soft crayon or felt-tipped pen, forming the words neatly and clearly.

The dictated account should have a title to illustrate that written materials have headings to show what they are about. A title will also serve to distinguish the story from other dictated accounts produced in the classroom. Titles can be obtained in different ways. Whatever procedure is used, undue time should not be devoted to title selection since this goal is not as important as the actual dictating and reading of the story.

Some groups may have difficulty thinking of a title, in which case the teacher may provide the titles for a number of experience stories until the children grasp the concept of what a title is. For instance, the teacher might say, "We will start our story with a title. The title will tell what our story is about. Since our story will be about the hamsters we just looked at, we will call our story 'The Hamsters.'" The title can then be written at the top of the chart and the dictation can proceed.

The teacher may, on the other hand, want the children to think of a title and may ask the group for suggestions. If a number of suggestions are given, the teacher may either select one to use or may ask the children to vote on the one they like best. Giving the children the opportunity to think of a title provides a chance for them to generalize from the points covered in the discussion. Such generalization requires children to deal with main ideas, a valuable comprehension skill that will prepare them for grasping main ideas in later reading materials.

In most circumstances the title should be decided upon before the account is dictated, so that the topic is clearly defined. A pre-selected title can help the group stay on the topic while dictating. There are times, however, when discussion of the title can be delayed until the whole story has been dictated. The group can read the whole story aloud and then decide on a title. This procedure requires a different skill—verbalizing the main idea of what has been dictated, as opposed to summarizing the discussion. By occasionally using this procedure, the teacher can help the pupils generalize from the details included in the story, another way of building skill in getting the main idea.

Once the title has been obtained, the group should be told that they will compose a story about the item that has just been discussed. Introductory comments like the following can be used:

> We all noticed lots of interesting things about the _____. Now we are ready to write a story about what we saw. Think of what you would like to say about the _____. I will write your ideas on the chart. Who would like to begin?

It is not necessary for each child in the group to contribute an idea. Once the story has been completed, all the children in the group will have a chance to become quite familiar with it and thus to feel that it is theirs. In a group of six to eight children only four or five may actually contribute ideas, and this should be considered quite acceptable. The teacher should, in fact, take care to hold the story to a reasonable length so that the reading demands are not unduly frustrating to the group.

"Reasonable" story length can vary from group to group. In a very immature group or in one with limited oral language facility, the dictated story will probably be briefer than with a more mature group of children. Teachers must gauge the optimum length of a dictated story by the needs and abilities of the children with whom they are working. The elements to consider are the children's

1. Oral language facility
2. Willingness to dictate
3. Attention span
4. Ability to learn to reread the story

We have observed that the average story length seems to be a running word count of twenty-five to forty words. Stories within this range usually cover one side of one page of chart paper.

For an effective recording of the story the following procedures may be used:

1. Record each child's statement immediately after it has been given, repeating the words while writing them on the chart.
2. Focus the group's attention on the chart during recording so that the children will see the individual words formed and will note the left-right progression of the formation of words and sentences.
3. Include the children's names with the statements they make (The children's names are often the easiest words for them to learn to recognize. In addition, their names serve as aids to remembering what statements were included in the story and so further enable the reading of the story to proceed with ease.) Most teachers find it preferable to begin the statement with the child's name, e.g., *Mark said, "The shells are pink and shiny."* *
4. Include commas, quotation marks, and other appropriate punctuation with each statement.

*Once children have become familiar with the procedures for dictating stories and have made good progress in reading these stories and establishing word banks, the teacher will want to eliminate the names from the story. When names are dropped, the stories become more like formal reading materials and can help children make the transition into reading library books and other published works. Children's names are useful in the early stages of LEA but can often be dropped after several weeks of regular dictation.

5. At the completion of each statement direct attention to the chart and, pointing to the words, read the sentence aloud.
6. Do not put sentences on the chart in list form, one sentence per line. The first sentence should be indented, and each succeeding sentence begins where the previous sentence ends on the chart. This emphasizes the unity of the story and keeps the chart from looking like a large exercise sheet.
7. Space words and sentences carefully so that the chart as a whole is clear and readable.

Figure 1 illustrates a neat, attractive experience story that resulted from following these recommended procedures.

The teacher should be prepared to accept whatever contributions are made rather than try to influence the content, vocabulary, or order of ideas. It may be tempting to suggest that the children describe certain features of the stimulus, use certain words that were brought up in the discussion, or organize the story in a particular fashion, but the particular words, sentences, and sequence of ideas children use in their dictation are less important than what the children learn about the process of reading by dictating their ideas, seeing them recorded on paper, and reading the finished product. Thus, there is little cause for concern if the finished product seems somewhat disorganized by teacher standards or does not include all the points that were brought out in the preceding discussion.

We once saw a teacher and her pupils busily pacing off fifty feet along the school corridor. They had been talking about a whale shark that was fifty feet long, and they wanted to see how long that would actually be. We might have expected the ensuing story to have reflected this measure of the shark's size, since the activity had been so interesting to all. However, the following story was dictated:

SHARKS

The tiger shark is the meanest of them all.
The whale shark is nice and he eats little
fish. Sharks are big and little. The tiger
shark is mean. The dwarf shark is fat, and
he lives in Japan.

Although the teacher was surprised when nothing about the whale shark's size was dictated, the absence of this concept did not detract from the story's value for reading instruction.

> Snowfall
>
> In the day and in the night snow flakes come down. You can ski on the snow and go sledding. We can make snowballs and a snowman. Sometimes we make angels in the snow. Sometimes we make igloos. When there is snow, we can make snow ice cream.
>
> Story 14

Figure 1: Experience story

Dictated stories rarely reflect all the preceding oral language activity. Instead, the maturity and interests of the children usually determine what is dictated. This is not to discount the value of the oral language experience but rather to emphasize that all the ideas discussed need not be recorded. If the completed story represents the children's ideas phrased in their language, the story can profitably be used for reading instruction.

Besides accepting ideas, the teacher should also accept and record each contribution in the exact language each child uses. That is, if a child uses a particular dialect pattern, colloquial expression, incorrect grammatical construction, or sentence fragment, it should be accepted and recorded without comment as to its anomalous nature.

Many teachers at first object to this practice, believing that only Standard English should be allowed in experience stories. Their reasoning is that children need to learn correct language usage and that accepting incorrect or non-Standard statements will only reinforce their continued use.

We argue for the complete acceptance of children's language for the following reasons:

1. The major objective of using experience stories is to teach children to process written language, i.e., to read. Changing the children's language patterns can confuse pupils as they attempt to attach meaning to the written word. To illustrate how this confusion can occur, we offer the following situation, which we observed first hand. A teacher was taking dictation on the topic of what some children had done over a holiday weekend. One child said, "Me and my mom went to Philadelphia." The teacher, concerned about the usage error, said, "That's fine, but we must put it down the right way." The teacher corrected the statement orally and then wrote the correction on the chart: *My mom and I went to Philadelphia*. When the group attempted to read the chart story, most of the children "read" what they had first heard and what they were most likely to have said—"Me and my mom"—as the teacher pointed to the words *My mom and I*. The confusion was evident as the teacher continually attempted to correct their language while some of the children continued to state the idea in the original words and others tried to follow the teacher. And, of course, there was confusion in the associations many were making with the first four words, saying *me* for *my*, and *and* for *mom*, etc.

2. Errors or idiosyncrasies in language usage do not necessarily reflect errors in the communication of ideas. If the group and the teacher know what the "erring" child means, the process of communication has been effective and the written material (the chart story) is seen as a meaningful piece by everyone involved.

3. Language usage can be refined and "corrected" in other areas of the school curriculum, at other times of the day, if such goals are considered important. As children begin to improve oral language facility, they will generally start to use correct patterns in their dictation as well. Thus, if early dictated stories reveal anomalies of language, further instruction and communication experiences in other classroom situations can reduce these problems.

Although we advise not changing pupil language during the course of dictation, we have found that teachers can do much to shape and refine the children's language during discussion and dictation, often eliminating the need to reject contributions because the language is inappropriate. Also, by refining techniques for eliciting story contributions, teachers can help children gradually improve the vocabulary and sentence variety of their dictations. Two examples of dictations taken by different teachers from the same group of students illustrate that different methods of taking dictation can result in very different stories.

On October 22, a group of children dictated this story to their teacher:

SPIDERS ARE UGLY

A spider has eight legs. A wolf spider is
ugly. Spider webs are sticky. Black widows
are the deadliest spiders in the United
States. They spin a web to make a home
and to catch their prey. When baby
spiders are big, they break out of their
egg sac.

On November 28, the same children dictated this story to a student teacher:

PINEAPPLES ARE GOOD

Pineapples are juicy. Pineapples are
delicious. Pineapples come from Hawaii.
Pineapples are sweet. The pineapples are
good. Pineapples are round.

The two stories are so different in vocabulary and sentence structure that it almost seems as if they were dictated by two different groups rather than by the same group. Or it may seem as if the group somehow regressed during the month's lapse between the two stories. The difference, however, was in the teachers' methods of eliciting dictation.

The student teacher had removed the pineapple and grouped the children around the chart, saying only, "Tell me what to write." Once one child "set the pattern," the others followed along, and the story followed a listlike form with very little variety. In contrast, after removing the stimulus, the classroom teacher had continued the oral discussion. When she heard a substantive comment, she said, "That's a good idea. Say it again while I write it on the chart." The discussion, with interruptions for recording interesting statements, had then continued until the chart was filled.

Probably some experience with recording dictation is necessary before a teacher can record selectively during a summary discussion. Nevertheless, this incident illustrates the teacher's important role in eliciting and shaping an interesting, informative chart story that reflects children's spoken language. Such a procedure can also be used to help children compose a story in Standard English if that is a major goal. The teacher can listen for appropriate contributions and can avoid using inappropriate ones without actually rejecting some children's contributions.

READING THE STORY

Once the story has been recorded, it should be read aloud several times before the session is over. The teacher should read the entire story once to the children first and then have the group read the story aloud together. After several group choral readings individual children can be encouraged to read the story alone while the rest of the group listens and follows visually. With each rereading, whether group or individual, the teacher should also join in the reading, setting the pace for the children. It may be tempting during these first readings to pause expectantly for children to read a word or a sentence without help, but such a strategy can be frustrating to the group. By always reading the story with the children and supplying words quickly when needed, the teacher will enable the reading to proceed smoothly and thus make the experience of reading pleasant and easy.

The experience story should be read with natural phrasing and pacing throughout. It should not be processed as if it were a word list, with unnaturally long pauses between words. Instead, the teacher and children should read it as a series of meaningful statements at a steady rate. We have found it helpful for the teacher to point (by hand or with a pointer) to indicate the words as they are read aloud. This helps to direct attention to the proper place on the chart and further emphasizes the necessary left-right progression of reading. By moving the pointer steadily across the lines, rather than pointing noticeably to one word at a time, the teacher will be able to retain a smooth and natural pacing during the reading.

The repeated reading of the experience story allows the children to begin the process of establishing a sight vocabulary. It is true that these first "readings" are essentially based on the children's memory for the dictated statements and on following the teacher's leading voice. However, with each repetition the children have the opportunity to make the associations between the spoken and written words which are the basis of learning to recognize the words in any context and in isolation. Each time the story is read, the teacher will notice the group gaining confidence and becoming familiar with more and more individual words and statements. Some children may read faster, trying to get ahead of the group to show that they know words or statements. Some, when reading alone with the teacher, will show marked independence from teacher help, setting the pace rather than following the teacher. Whenever the group or individuals show the ability to continue on their own, the teacher can allow them to do so, chiming in again only when the readers hesitate.

Of course, many children will not be able to read the entire story on their own at the end of this first series of repeated readings, nor is it expected that they will have solidly established any particular number of words as well-known sight words. In a typical lesson the children will have had six to ten opportunities to read through the whole story. (The teacher will have read it to the group once; the group will have read it three or four times; several, if not all, of the children will have read it individually with the teacher.) This number of repetitions, though substantial, will not be enough to enable children to learn all the words in a single story. Other rereadings and word-study activities are required to assure the establishment of words as sight words. However, providing numerous repetitions of the story at this point will make it relatively easy for most children to profit from the next steps in the procedure and to begin to learn a number of words.

CONDUCTING IMMEDIATE FOLLOW-UP ACTIVITIES

By the time the discussion, dictation, and repeated readings of the story have been completed, approximately half an hour will have gone by. The children will have had the opportunity to begin to learn some words from the story. A few minutes of word-study exercises at the end of the lesson will help reinforce these first learnings.

As we mentioned, rereading the story only begins to establish a sight vocabulary. Children will have relied on auditory memory and teacher guidance to accomplish their initial readings. However, they can only be said to *know* words when they can identify those words in a variety of contexts and in isolation. Some simple exercises done at this time will give them a chance to deal with story words in various stages of isolation and to begin to use story context as a help in figuring out some unknown words. We recommend using some or all of the following exercises; they are listed below in order, from recognizing a word in story context to reading a word in isolation.

1. Ask the children to find a particular word in the story; e.g., ask, "Who can find the word fuzzy?" Choose words that can be located easily either because of their high meaning value or because of their prominent positions on the chart. Have volunteers go to the chart and point to the given word.
2. If a word occurs more than once in the story, have children find it as many places as they can.
3. Point to a word in the dictated story. See if anyone can say it. If no one knows the word, move the pointer to the first word in that sentence. Pace the children's oral reading of the whole sentence, including the unknown word. Then point to the word again and ask, "What is it?"
4. Print a word from the story on the chalkboard. Choose one that will probably be easy to identify, e.g., someone's name, a key word from the title, or an unusual word from the body of the story. Ask for volunteers to identify the word as they look at it on the board. If it is identified, choose another word and see if it can be identified. When a word is not readily identified, give assistance in this sequence.
    a. Have someone locate the word in the story. Indicate the line in the story where the word appears if there is any difficulty.
    b. Pace oral rereading of the sentence up to the point at which the word occurs. See if the children can complete the sentence on their own and thus identify the word.
    c. Point to the word on the chalkboard and ask again, "What does it say?"

All these exercises help children direct attention to individual words. Also, the sequence in which the teacher provides assistance in figuring out unknown words demonstrates the usefulness of context clues. Children are able to see that using the story context is a way they can identify unfamiliar words.

Of course, the ultimate goal is recognizing words in a variety of new contexts, not just learning to recognize words in isolation. Thus, the teacher may also give children the opportunity to find key story words in selected materials that are made available soon after the immediate follow-up activities are completed. The teacher can have on hand several topic-related materials and can choose a few that contain story words at this time. For instance, several library books on snakes can be shown after a snake story, or a captioned picture of a Canada goose can be introduced after a Canada goose story. Children can look for newly learned words with helpful hints from the teacher as to the words' locations.

Only by working with a group and observing their abilities will a teacher be able to judge what kind of reinforcement exercises are needed. Some children within a group may be able to handle more difficult exercises while other children need to be given simpler reinforcement tasks, so different tasks can be given to different children. In general, the exercises should allow plenty of opportunity for success. A child should not be embarrassed in any way, and all efforts should be rewarded with praise for a good try even if the result is inaccurate. The point of doing exercises of this kind at this time is simply to provide *some* opportunities to deal with *some* words in relative isolation and in new contexts. A few moments can be used for these activities, and, as with other phases of the lesson, this last step should also be perceived by the children as being pleasant and easy.

DEVELOPING BASIC SKILLS

Once an experience story has been obtained, many opportunities must be provided to reinforce the sight vocabulary acquired from that story. Also, regular lessons and activities in word-attack skills and comprehension must be planned as follow-ups to the original story. It is relatively easy to obtain a dictated chart story and reread it with a group. However, this is only the first step in developing reading skills in a language-experience program. Related reading-skill activities using story books, word cards, and word banks must be developed from the dictated story charts. The quality and quantity of these related skill activities will determine the success of this approach as a procedure for teaching beginning reading. Specific plans for skill development are given in chapter 4. Here we will describe the materials that are used in the skill-development phase of the program.

Story Charts

The original chart is, of course, an important material that will be used for a variety of activities and therefore should be retained in the classroom. Many teachers find it useful to hang the obtained charts in chronological order on a chart rack. The charts are then readily available for rereading by children and for various teacher-directed activities, which we will describe in detail in chapter 4.

Figure 2:   Chart rack

Story Books

Very soon after a group has dictated a story and read it from the chart with teacher help, children should be given their own copies of the story. Because these copies will be used for a variety of skill activities it is important to provide a neat, clear copy for each child. We recommend that the teacher type (primer-type size) or neatly print the story on a spirit duplicator master and run off a copy for each child in the group. Additional copies can be made to use for independent activities, for the teacher to keep in a file, or for a group story book to be made available at the library table. (See Appendix A for directions on book binding.)

Some teachers like to hand out copies of a story in the afternoon if the dictation was obtained in the morning. Others prefer giving the copies to the children the day after the story has been dictated. Children should receive their individual copies of the story no later than this, however. Copies should be distributed soon so that sight words can be reinforced right away by rereading the story and completing other skill-development activities.

It is advisable to have a story book for each child so that num-

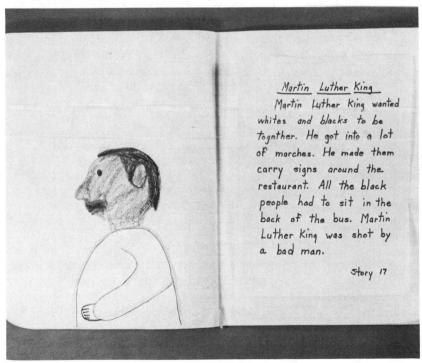

Figure 3:   Open story book

bered and dated stories can be kept neatly arranged in chronological order. The most useful story book arrangement we have seen is a firmly bound standard composition book in which the stories can be pasted or stapled after having been cut down to size. With this type of book each story can be fastened to one side of the page and the facing page used for the child's own illustration of the story.

When a group is given their copies of the dictated story, the following tasks need to be completed:

1. *The story should be fastened in the story books in the proper place*. Some teachers prefer to fasten the stories in the children's books for them. Others have the children do this. If the children are to place their stories in their own books, the teacher may need to guide the cutting, positioning, and fastening a few times. Cutting guidelines may be drawn on the master around the story to help the children cut the paper to fit the size of the book.
2. *The children should be directed to draw a picture on the facing page to go with the story*. The children's illustrations serve to make their story books attractive and unique, and the children usually enjoy the task. Further, an illustration distinguishes a story from the other stories in a book and is often used as a guide for finding that particular story again at a later time. Also, as children illustrate their stories, they will think again about the object or event that was the topic of dictation; the thinking and drawing thus help to prepare for later rereadings of the story. Finally, by later examining the children's illustrations, a teacher can gain information about individuals' general levels of maturity, attention to detail, and interpretation of the topic. Thus, story illustrations are useful in many ways and should always be included in this phase of the procedure.

Once the story has been put in the story book and a picture has been drawn to accompany it, the child has the basic reading materials on which many activities will be based.

Establishing a Word Bank

A major goal in any reading program is the development of the child's sight vocabulary. In a language-experience program this goal is accomplished through the use of a word bank, a collection of word cards that represents the child's sight vocabulary. Each child has a word bank; words are put in the word bank in the following manner:

1. *Reading the story—underlining words (I)*. When the children are given their copies of the dictated story, they should be di-

rected to read through the story and underline any words they know. This exercise reinforces the sight vocabulary that was acquired when the group read the story with teacher help. Most children will be able to recognize one or more words on this first recontact with the story. Often children's names, key nouns, or words in prominent positions, such as title words or the last word, will be recognized and underlined.

This exercise should be done without help from other children or the teacher. The object is for each child independently to indicate what is known with certainty. Children should not, however, be expected to know all the words in the story, or even most of the words. If the teacher makes these standards clear, children will feel comfortable working independently and noncompetitively, underlining only those words they know for sure.

2. *Reading the story with others.* Once children have worked with their own copies of the story to underline known words, they should be encouraged to read the story again with other children. The teacher may reconvene the group to reread the story from the original chart, following the procedures outlined ear-

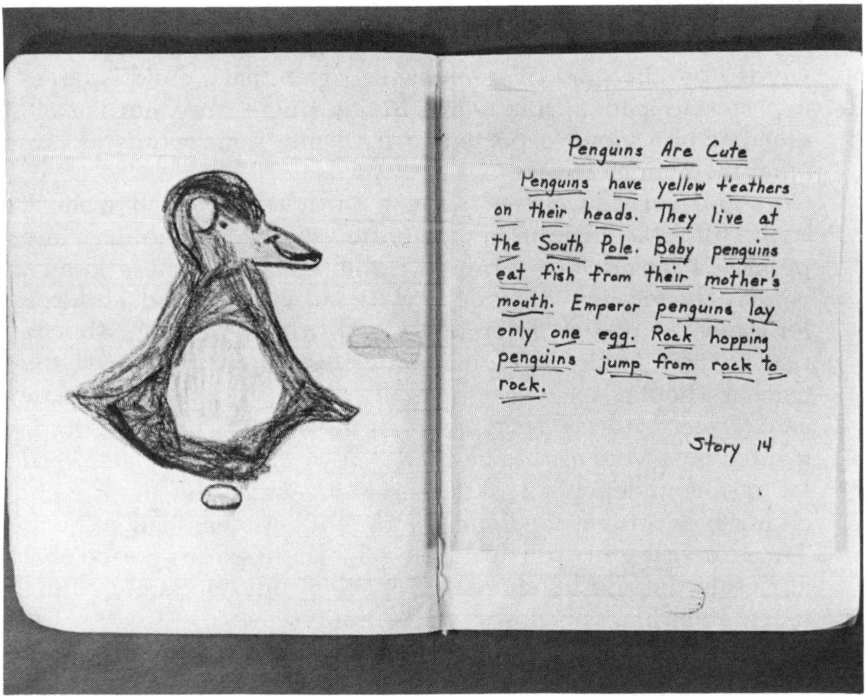

Figure 4:   Child's story with drawing

lier. Or the teacher may suggest that children pair up with a series of partners; each team so formed can take turns reading their copies of the story to each other. By thus working together children can help each other identify words that are not immediately recognized. Repeated perusal of the story will continue to reinforce already known words and can encourage the learning of additional words. Of course, some children will proceed by identifying single known words rather than reading each word in the story.

3. *Rereading the story—underlining words (II).* After some additional group rereadings of the experience story the children should be given a second opportunity to work independently with the dictated story. Using the same copies they worked with earlier, they should be directed to read through the story again, underlining any words they know with certainty, putting a second line under words previously known and still known and a single line under "new" known words.

By the time children have worked with their stories to underline known words twice and have reread their stories independently and with each other, they will have had many opportunities to learn to recognize some of the words in the dictated story. In most instances two or three days of working with the dictated story will suffice for children to acquire some sight words from the story. We emphasize again that a child is never expected to learn *all* the words in any single story, nor is each member of a group expected to learn the same words as any other member or members.

4. *Checking learned words.* Finally, the teacher will need to check each child's acquisition and retention of sight vocabulary and provide a means for continued reinforcement of these known words. The teacher will need to work individually with children for a few minutes to determine which words they actually can read at sight. Using the child's underlined copy of the story, the teacher should isolate each underlined word with a window card. Each word the child can read in isolation, i.e., at sight, is printed on a word card to be filed in a word bank and later used for various independent skill activities. A group of six or eight children can be checked one at a time in less than half an hour. Time can be taken to do this during the language arts period or at any other time during the day. Teachers' aides or parent volunteers can also check known words in this way.

At the end of this checking period, each child should have been able to acquire one or more word cards, representing

Figure 5:   Story and window card

known words. It is important to make sure that the children
know well the words that are put on word cards. Later exercises
with word cards can be done successfully with known words but
can be frustrating with many unknown words. When using the
window card, the checker should only make word cards for
words that are recognized immediately and firmly without
teacher help. If there is real uncertainty or long hesitation over a
word (even if it is underlined twice), the checker should not
make a word card for that word. Only those words that are underlined should be checked. It is important to respect children's
underlining, reinforcing a growing sense of responsibility for
their own learning. It may be tempting to urge children to "try"
words that are not underlined, but we have found that this can
lead to children underlining more words than they know with
certainty in order to please the teacher. It is better to put a few
well-learned words in a word bank (and even some of these may
be forgotten in time) than to put in many words that may be
quickly forgotten.

5. *Constructing word cards.* Word cards need to be sturdy enough
to withstand handling. They can be made either of oaktag or the

lightweight cardboard of file cards. Word cards also need to be small enough to arrange in lists or sentences on desktops, yet large enough for small fingers to manipulate. A size of 1" × 1½" works quite well. (See Figure 6 for an illustration of word cards.)

Some teachers like to prepare hundreds of blank word cards by cutting blocks of oaktag into 1" × 1½" pieces. We have seen others who prepared a spirit duplicator master with lines to make 5" × 8" file cards in squares of 1" × 1½". The cards were then cut apart as they were given to the children.

As children receive their word cards, they write their initials and the story number on the back of each card. Should the word be forgotten, the story number will make it possible to locate the original story context. The initials will provide ready proof of ownership in the event of spilled or mixed-up word cards.

Maintaining a Word Bank

Children's word cards should be stored in a sturdy container. A standard 3" × 5" file box is probably the most useful accessory for

Figure 6:   Word cards

this purpose. Initially the word cards can simply be placed in the file box without regard for any particular organizational scheme. By the time that a word bank includes about thirty words, however, it becomes necessary to organize the word cards in some way. Otherwise, children may become quite frustrated as they look for a particular word in a desk-top pile of many words. The best organization of word cards is alphabetical. Using this scheme serves two purposes: children have a manageable system for sorting and retrieving word cards and at the same time learn alphabetical order in a functional manner.

A set of alphabetized cards designed for file boxes is needed to organize the word cards alphabetically. The word bank is arranged with each alphabet card followed by a small envelope containing all the words that begin with that letter. The envelope should be marked with the letter, both capital and lower case. In addition there should be an envelope marked "I forgot." This envelope can be used to store a few words that may be forgotten over time and need to be reviewed before being placed again in a regular word card envelope.

The word bank with its store of word cards, the children's story books, and the dictated story chart constitute the primary materials for developing reading skills in a language-experience program. Use of these materials in the skill-development program will be described further in subsequent chapters.

SUMMARY

There are five steps in the basic procedure of obtaining a dictated story and developing instructional materials and skill-training activities related to the story. The sample weekly plan below provides an overview of how these steps might be scheduled for one group of children.

Monday
Discussion of stimulus
Taking dictation
Rereading story
Immediate follow-up activities

Tuesday
Rereading story
Underlining known words (I)
Illustrating story
Teacher-directed follow-up activities

Wednesday
Underlining known words (II)
Teacher-directed follow-up activities
Independent follow-up activities

Thursday
Independent follow-up activities
Teacher checking of known words
Making word cards

Friday
Catch-up activities, such as finishing word cards
Independent activities, word-card games
Review of word-bank cards

This schedule is not meant to be a plan to be followed rigidly. We present it only to provide an overview of a week's work with one group and to illustrate the chronological order in which the basic steps are to be implemented. Of course, the independent and teacher-directed skill activities included in the group's program will vary each day. These activities will include skill lessons using the story chart and other materials, rereading of current and past dictated stories, and various word-bank activities. Methods for implementing these additional procedures are explained in chapter 4.

Chapter III

Grouping
for
Instruction

The language-experience approach is an individualized reading program in that children are allowed to develop reading skills at their own rates of learning. However, children do not necessarily work individually. While lessons may be planned for individual children, a class is usually organized into small groups for instructional purposes. Individualization occurs within the group as each child learns from an activity what he is ready to learn. For example, in a skill lesson to develop the concept of forming plurals, one child may remember the examples as sight words while another child will be able to generalize to recognizing regular plural forms. There are no absolute expectations of how much a single child should learn in any one lesson. Thus, one child may learn ten sight words one day while another child in the same group learns five. Both will have been successful; both will have profited from one another's contributions to the group; both will feel a sense of accomplishment.

Most often instructional groups should be fairly homogeneous in terms of pupils' achievement levels, i.e., six or eight children of about the same level of achievement grouped together. Instruction will meet children's needs most efficiently if several children are ready for the same lesson at the same time, a situation that frequently arises when children of the same achievement level are working together. Also, in such a homogeneous group, children will have fairly equal chances to be successful in relation to their group mates. No one will consistently learn more quickly or more slowly than others in the group.

There are times, however, when heterogeneous groups can and should be formed. Heterogeneous grouping can be particularly beneficial when some children in the group are more limited in oral language abilities and background of experience. The richer oral language of the more able pupils can serve as a model for the less able children. In addition, the group as a whole will reflect a wider, more diverse background of experience as ideas and comments are exchanged in discussion and recorded during dictation. Cross-achievement-level grouping is also beneficial when children of varying achievement levels need extra practice in the same skill. And again there are times when altering group membership can provide a needed change of pace. Thus, there may be a variety of reasons for grouping children heterogeneously at different times, and this is readily accomplished in a language-experience program.

Individualization within groups combined with flexible grouping patterns allows for maximum individualization in a language-experience program. Flexible grouping also discourages the static grouping patterns that so often arise when a typical basal program is used and children are kept in their original groups for months at a time or even for the entire school year. In a language-experience program, because all children dictate, establish word banks, and engage in similar word-recognition skill activities, children can easily be moved from one instructional group to another. Transfers to different groups can be made periodically without the difficulties that such moves cause in basal programs when different groups are using different books and possibly different instructional procedures. Frequent regrouping for various purposes can also reduce the status associated with relatively permanent groups; i.e., in a well-run language-experience classroom, "Bluebirds" and "Robins," top groups and low groups, are not as evident since everyone is learning together in varying group combinations throughout the year.

In the first few weeks of school it is necessary to assess individuals' strengths and weaknesses in order to establish initial homogeneous instructional groups. Teachers need to observe the behaviors and attitudes that provide clues to children's readiness for formal reading instruction using language-experience procedures. Some children will have come to school already reading; others may not have established any skills beyond the ability to recognize a few individual letters. The best way to make these

diagnostic observations is to involve children directly in the processes of dictating experience stories and rereading these with
teacher help. That is, the best way to judge how well children will
profit from a language-experience program is to involve them immediately in the program and observe what they are able to accomplish. Scores on standardized reading-readiness tests will not provide the best information at this point, although such information
may be considered as grouping decisions are made. Several days of
observation will probably be needed before the first regular instructional groups are established. There are two different
strategies for accomplishing this initial diagnosis and forming instructional groups: use of group-dictated stories and use of
individual-dictated stories.

USING GROUP DICTATION FOR DIAGNOSTIC PURPOSES

To begin informal assessment using group dictation, the
teacher should group children randomly for the first week's activities. Three or four groups should be formed, each including six to
eight children. The teacher will need to work with each group for
several days during the first week in order to assess individuals'
strengths and weaknesses. These work periods will also familiarize
the children with basic procedures used in the language-
experience program. Since these initial groups are temporary, the
teacher does not need to establish any particular identity for the
groups; e.g., the members do not need to decide on a name for the
group.

During this first week, the teacher should work with each
group to obtain a dictated story and observe the children's abilities
to reread the story and participate in various skill lessons relating to
the story. These activities will allow the teacher to note children's
strengths and weaknesses in reading and reading-readiness skills.
Specific procedures for obtaining and working with a dictated story
have been explained fully in chapter 2. The first four steps in this
basic procedure should be followed at this stage. The fifth step,
intended to provide children with intensive skill training once instructional groups have been established, is usually omitted during
the initial diagnostic stage.

As children discuss a stimulus, dictate, and reread an experience story, the teacher should note children's oral language facility,
attentiveness to different aspects of the lesson, and ability to reread
the dictation and identify individual words. The significant be-

haviors can be organized into a simple checklist which the teacher can use to assess each child in the group. A sample checklist is given in Table 1.

Each temporary group should go through a group discussion of a stimulus and should dictate and reread an experience story so that the teacher will have the opportunity to assess each child in the class. The teacher, of course, may need to reconvene each group two or three times over a period of two to three days to reread their story since every child in a group cannot be observed at one sitting.

To illustrate the kinds of judgments that can be made in this way, we will compare the checklists of three different children and elaborate on the behaviors and attitudes that each child revealed over three days' time. (See Tables 2, 3, and 4.)

Luke showed obvious interest in the gerbil that was used as a stimulus for his group's dictated story. He picked the gerbil up to pet it and commented on the color and texture of the animal's fur. He asked questions about the gerbil's food preferences and wanted to know how much the animal would eat. He listened to other children's comments and occasionally added his own observations to someone else's. He was not very attentive during the recording of the story, seeming to be more interested in peeking at the gerbil, which had been placed behind the teacher on a table. He did watch carefully, however, when his own name and contribution were written on the chart, and when the story was completed, he did pay attention to the written account as the teacher read it to the group.

Luke's oral language was generally quite good. He volunteered comments and responded eagerly to teacher questions about what he noticed in the gerbil's cage. During the discussion he used a number of well-formed sentences, e.g., "He's brown and white like a hamster." "He feels furry." "How much of this stuff does he eat?" "What's his name?" His contribution to the experience story was, "His fur is soft and brown."

When the teacher encouraged the group to reread the dictated account, Luke chimed in with others and attempted to read the whole story. He also volunteered to reread the story individually with teacher help and remained attentive throughout this task. He was not able to read any of the story independently though he repeated all the words as he followed the teacher's lead. He raised his hand repeatedly when the teacher pointed to various words in the story to have them identified, and he was able to identify his own name and the word *gerbil*.

In the two days after the initial dictation, Luke showed the

Table 1
LEA Readiness Checklist

Name _____

Date _____

Attention

    1. Shows interest in stimulus   _____

    2. Follows discussion of stimulus   _____

    3. Watches recording of dictated story   _____

    4. Looks at dictated story during rereading   _____

Oral language

    1. Comments on stimulus during discussion   _____

    2. Can speak in complete sentences   _____

    3. Good vocabulary and sentence structure   _____

    4. Volunteers comments or speaks readily
        when spoken to   _____

Reading skills

    1. Attempts to reread story with group   _____

    2. Attempts to reread story individually with
        teacher help   _____

    3. Is able to read most or all of the story without
        teacher help   _____

    4. Shows interest in finding individual words
        in the story   _____

    5. Is able to identify individual words   _____

    6. Seeks to read chart story independently during
        free time   _____

    7. Shows interest in reading materials   _____

Comments

Table 2
Luke's LEA Readiness Checklist

Name ___Luke___

Date ___9/25___

Attention

　1. Shows interest in stimulus ✓

　2. Follows discussion of stimulus ✓

　3. Watches recording of dictated story ___

　4. Looks at dictated story during rereading ✓

Oral language

　1. Comments on stimulus during discussion ✓

　2. Can speak in complete sentences ✓

　3. Good vocabulary and sentence structure ✓

　4. Volunteers comments or speaks readily
　　when spoken to ✓

Reading skills

　1. Attempts to reread story with group ✓

　2. Attempts to reread story individually with
　　teacher help ✓

　3. Is able to read most or all of the story without
　　teacher help ___

　4. Shows interest in finding individual words
　　in the story ✓

　5. Is able to identify individual words ___

　6. Seeks to read chart story independently during
　　free time ___

　7. Shows interest in reading materials ___

Comments

same interests and abilities relating to the experience story when his group gathered together. He did not show particular interest in the chart story at other times, preferring to explore the room and engage in other activities, notably continuing to watch the gerbil. He showed mild interest in the books displayed on the library table but did not sit down to look through any books beyond examining a few pictures.

In general Luke shows numerous signs of being able to profit from formal reading instruction using the language-experience approach. His strength in oral language, his attentiveness during the rereading, and his ability to identify a few individual words all suggest that he is ready to begin and will probably learn rather easily.

Gary showed interest in the gerbil, petting the animal and smiling. He seemed to listen to the other children's comments about the gerbil but restricted his own communication to smiling at other children's remarks and uttering a word here and there. He lost interest in the activities when the gerbil was removed from sight and occupied himself by pulling at his shoelaces and playfully nudging another child who was sitting next to him. When the group reread the story with the teacher, Gary watched the teacher and the others in the group but did not pay attention to the story itself.

Gary's oral language was limited to one or two word statements, often repetitions of words that other children used, e.g., "gerbil," "cage," "food." When asked how he liked the gerbil, Gary responded by saying "yeah" and smiling. He did not contribute to the dictated account and shook his head when the teacher asked him if he wanted to add something.

When the teacher encouraged the group to reread the dictated account, Gary read along with the others for the first few words and then looked away from the chart to another part of the room where some children were gathered. He would look back at the chart story when reminded by the teacher but soon lost interest again. He did not volunteer to reread the story individually with the teacher and did not respond with interest or attention when the teacher asked for individual words to be identified.

In the two days after the initial dictation, Gary showed no interest in the dictated account or in other reading materials in the room. He continued to be relatively inattentive during the times the group was gathered around the story chart and was unable to read with the group or to identify individual words. He showed interest in some puzzles and manipulative toys in the room but typically lost interest in any activity after a few moments.

Table 3
Gary's LEA Readiness Checklist

Name ___GARY___

Date ___9/25___

Attention

    1. Shows interest in stimulus ___✓___

    2. Follows discussion of stimulus ___✓___

    3. Watches recording of dictated story _____

    4. Looks at dictated story during rereading _____

Oral language

    1. Comments on stimulus during discussion ___✓___

    2. Can speak in complete sentences _____

    3. Good vocabulary and sentence structure _____

    4. Volunteers comments or speaks readily
       when spoken to _____

Reading skills

    1. Attempts to reread story with group _____

    2. Attempts to reread story individually with
       teacher help _____

    3. Is able to read most or all of the story without
       teacher help _____

    4. Shows interest in finding individual words
       in the story _____

    5. Is able to identify individual words _____

    6. Seeks to read chart story independently during
       free time _____

    7. Shows interest in reading materials _____

Comments

Table 4
Sharon's LEA Readiness Checklist

Name __*Sharon*__

Date __*9|25*__

Attention

   1. Shows interest in stimulus ✓

   2. Follows discussion of stimulus ✓

   3. Watches recording of dictated story ✓

   4. Looks at dictated story during rereading ✓

Oral language

   1. Comments on stimulus during discussion ✓

   2. Can speak in complete sentences ✓

   3. Good vocabulary and sentence structure ✓

   4. Volunteers comments or speaks readily
      when spoken to ✓

Reading skills

   1. Attempts to reread story with group ✓

   2. Attempts to reread story individually with
      teacher help ✓

   3. Is able to read most or all of the story without
      teacher help ✓

   4. Shows interest in finding individual words
      in the story ✓

   5. Is able to identify individual words ✓

   6. Seeks to read chart story independently during
      free time ✓

   7. Shows interest in reading materials ✓

Comments

In general Gary's behavior suggests that he will need more time to develop oral language skills and increased ability to attend to reading and reading-related tasks before he will be able to read dictated accounts, learn individual words, and otherwise profit from formal reading instruction.

Sharon followed the discussion of the gerbil closely, listening to the teacher's and children's comments carefully and offering ideas of her own. She told the group about some gerbils she had once seen in a pet store and was particularly interested in where the teacher had obtained the class's gerbil. She was attentive throughout the discussion, dictating and rereading phases.

Sharon's oral language was rated superior by the teacher. Not only did Sharon use complete sentences, but her vocabulary and sentence structure were significantly advanced in comparison with others in the class; she also spoke fluently and at length when given the opportunity. For instance, she commented that the gerbil had "unusual colors" and that gerbils "make especially good pets because they're easy to take care of and do lots of interesting things."

Sharon did quite well on all the activities related to the reading of the dictated story. She read along with the group eagerly and was the first to volunteer to read the story individually. This she was able to do well on her own, needing the teacher's help with only two words in the story. She knew all the words the teacher asked her to identify in isolation as well.

In the two days following the initial dictation, Sharon returned to the chart story twice and read it aloud to other children who were also looking at it. In addition, she showed considerable interest in library materials during free time and was often engrossed in examining books around the room. The teacher discovered that Sharon could easily read one or two of the easy-to-read materials without any help.

In general Sharon shows well-developed abilities to read already. Her performance suggests that she will certainly respond well to formal reading instruction using the language-experience approach and will probably be ahead of her classmates for some time, if not throughout the school year.

USING INDIVIDUAL DICTATION FOR DIAGNOSTIC PURPOSES

A second initial diagnostic strategy that may be used is to obtain an individually dictated story from each child in the class, making necessary observations of skills and abilities in the process and analyzing certain components of the dictation.* This strategy involves more detailed analysis of prereading and reading skills and may require more time than the group-dictation diagnostic procedure, but it can also yield more information on each child's strengths and weaknesses.

The first requirement for implementing individual story diagnosis is to decide on one stimulus to use for all individually dictated stories. By using the same stimulus for each child, the procedures will be standardized, allowing for comparisons among pupils. A toy, a puppet, or some other colorful or interesting object is a good choice for a stimulus.

The teacher (or teacher's aide) should sit with each child in a relatively quiet place in the class, free from the distractions of the rest of the children's activities. The child should be shown the stimulus, allowed to handle it, and engaged in a brief conversation, prompted by teacher questions and comments. The amount of time spent on this initial conversation should be standardized from one pupil to the next; one minute is a good standard. Then the child should be asked to tell a story about the stimulus, and a two-minute language sample should be recorded by the teacher or teacher's aide as the child talks. The two minutes should be timed from the time the child begins talking. (Obtaining two-minute samples from each child will provide continued standardized conditions and allow for comparison among individuals.) If a child is talking when the two minutes are up, the teacher should continue recording until the child finishes the sentence and then stop the dictation. If the child pauses during the two minutes, the teacher should encourage continuation by saying something like, "Go ahead. Tell some more about _____." or "These are good ideas. Do you have some more to say?" The child should also be asked to give the story a title. After the child has finished dictating, the teacher should say, "What shall we call your story? Can you think of a title?" The title, if any is given, should be recorded at the top of the dictation.

Once the dictation has been completed, the teacher should call the child's attention to the written account and say, "Let's read your story together." The teacher should position the account so that both can see it clearly and should then read the entire story aloud once at a slow enough pace so that the child will be able to "read" along. The teacher should also point to the words while the oral

---

*This procedure was developed by Dr. Carol Dixon, Department of Education, University of California at Santa Barbara, and is being used here with her permission.

reading proceeds, just as is done in the first rereading of any dictated story. After the dictation and rereading have been completed, the child can be dismissed.

The next step involves analysis of the child's approach to this task and of the story itself. The checklist in Table 5 should be used for this analysis.*

The first section of the checklist should be completed as soon as the child has been dismissed, so that the child's behaviors are fresh in the teacher's mind. The last two sections can be completed later, perhaps after a number of stories from different children have been obtained.

We will illustrate the use of the checklist by analyzing one child's story that was obtained under the specified conditions. The teacher introduced a wooden marionette as the stimulus. The following story was obtained:

THE WOOD MAN

He jumps up and down. When you pull the
strings he jumps. Red. Blue. Black hat. I
can make him dance on the table. He has
a stick in his hand.

To score Mary's checklist, the number of checks in each column of each section was counted and entered on the line marked "Column Totals." These column totals were then multiplied by the respective weights (3, 2, or 1). The resulting products were then added to obtain the subtotal in each section. These subtotals were then added together to obtain the "grand total"—in Mary's case, 25. Suggested criteria for using the checklist are as follows:

Grand total: 17 or below   Child is not ready for
                               formal reading instruction

Grand total: 17–27   Child is ready for
                               formal reading instruction

Grand total: 27 or above   Child probably possesses
                               some reading skills already

These criteria can be used to form initial homogeneous instructional groups. However, as Dixon recognizes, the criteria should be used with caution; more research needs to be done before firm decisions can be made about grouping first graders on this basis. Teachers using the checklist and described procedures may need to

Table 5
Language-Experience Checklist

	Weighted Point Value		
	3	2	1
Observable behaviors			
1. Paces dictation to transcriber	usually	sometimes	seldom
2. Pauses at end of phrase or sentence	usually	sometimes	seldom
3. Reads back correctly	most	some	none
Column Totals	_____	_____	_____
	3 × _____	2 × _____	1 × _____
	Observable subtotal _____		

	3	2	1
Global language usage:			
1. Complete sentences	all	some	none
2. Total words	31+	16–30	0–15
3. Average words per sentence	9+	4–8	0–3
4. Total different words	30+	16–30	1–15
Column Totals	_____	_____	_____
	3 × _____	2 × _____	1 × _____
	Global subtotal _____		

	3	2	1
Refined language usage:			
1. Number of adjectives	9+	4–8	0–3
2. Number of adverbs	3+	1–2	0
3. Number of prepositional phrases	4+	1–3	0
4. Number of embedded sentences	2+	1	0
Column Totals	_____	_____	_____
	3 × _____	2 × _____	1 × _____
	Refined subtotal _____		
	Grand total _____		

*This checklist is an unpublished revision of a checklist that was originally presented by Dr. Dixon in *Language Arts* 54 (May 1977), 5:501–505. It is used by permission.

Table 6
Mary's Language-Experience Checklist

	Weighted Point Value		
	3	2	1
Observable behaviors			
1. Paces dictation to transcriber	usually	✓ sometimes	seldom
2. Pauses at end of phrase or sentence	✓ usually	sometimes	seldom
3. Reads back correctly	most	✓ some	none
Column Totals	1	2	0
	3 × 1	2 × 2	1 × 0
Observable subtotal	7		
Global language usage:			
1. Complete sentences	all	✓ some	none
2. Total words	✓ 31+	16–30	0–15
3. Average words per sentence	9+	✓ 4–8	0–3
4. Total different words	✓ 30+	16–30	1–15
Column Totals	2	2	0
	3 × 2	2 × 2	1 × 0
Global subtotal	10		
Refined language usage:			
1. Number of adjectives	9+	✓ 4–8	0–3
2. Number of adverbs	3+	✓ 1–2	0
3. Number of prepositional phrases	4+	✓ 1–3	0
4. Number of embedded sentences	2+	✓ 1	0
Column Totals	0	4	0
	3 × 0	2 × 4	1 × 0
Refined subtotal	8		
Grand total	25		

Comments:

Global language usage: (1) *Red. Blue. Black hat.* are not considered complete sentences. (2) 34 total words. (3) Average words per sentence = 7. (4) 30 different words. *Jump* and *jumps* are counted as two different words.

Refined languages usage: (1) 8 adjectives: *the, wood, the , red, blue, black, the, his.* (2) 2 adverbs: *up, down.* (3) 2 prepositional phrases: *on the table, in his hand.* (4) 1 embedded sentence: *when you pull the strings.* . . .

modify the criteria according to their own observations and judgments. Whether the criteria are too stringent or not stringent enough can only be determined by using the checklist, making grouping decisions, and judging how reasonable these decisions actually seem to be.

SUMMARY

The purposes of grouping in a language-experience program are twofold. Grouping can provide an efficient means for teaching reading skills when children have similar reading-skill-development needs. Grouping can also foster language development while permitting an interchange of ideas and experience. We see grouping as a flexible procedure that can range from individually dictated stories with grouping for skill development to large-group discussion experiences followed by homogeneous small-group dictation. Flexible grouping can therefore provide for efficient classroom organization while meeting individual needs.

Chapter IV

Teaching and Reinforcing Skills

Dictating and rereading dictated stories are the first steps in an LEA program, but these activities alone will not provide for adequate development of reading ability. A strong LEA program includes a wide variety of skill lessons to reinforce sight vocabulary and develop use of word-analysis and comprehension skills. The skill-development phase of the program will be most effective when skill lessons are related to the dictated stories' content and vocabulary and are planned to meet specific, observed pupil needs. Such activities may immediately follow dictation, may occur later in the same day, or may be planned for subsequent days. We have observed that immersion in well-designed skill-development activities is one key to children's success in an LEA program.

In this chapter we will describe a variety of teacher-directed activities and independent tasks that can be used to reinforce and refine reading skills. Suggestions for planning will be given at the end of the chapter.

TEACHER-DIRECTED ACTIVITIES

Reading instruction that follows the dictation of an experience story can be divided into three categories:

1. Increasing sight vocabulary
2. Teaching word-attack skills
3. Refining reading comprehension.

These skills are usually integrated into lessons in some way, however. A lesson designed to increase sight vocabulary can affect comprehension of what is read; a word-attack skill lesson will inevitably involve reinforcement of sight vocabulary. The following exchange, for instance, illustrates one type of lesson that can follow dictation. In this lesson, based on the dictated story "Elephants," a number of different skills may be developed.

ELEPHANTS

The elephant is grown when he is fifteen
years old. Elephants throw dirt on
themselves to keep from getting sunburn.
Elephants put water on themselves.
Elephants eat rice and bananas.

Teacher: (Writes the word *water* on the chalkboard.) Who can find this word in the story? (Visual discrimination.)

Joe: Here. (Points to the word *water*.)

T: Do you know what the word says? (The children hesitate.)

T: Let's start at the beginning of the sentence and read together. (Pointing to the first word of the sentence in which *water* occurs, the teacher paces choral reading through the sentence.) (Use of context clues.)

C: Elephants put water on themselves.

T: (Points to the word *water* written on the chalkboard.) What's this word? (Reinforcing sight vocabulary.)

C: Water.

T: (Underlines the *w*.) What's the name of this letter? (Letter recognition.)

C: W.

T: (Points to the *w*.) Listen to the word I'm going to say. Does it have the same beginning sound as water? Watch. (Auditory discrimination.)

C: Yes.

T: Does *will* have the same beginning sound as *water*?

C: Yes.

T: Does *father* have the same beginning sound as *water*?

C: No.

T: Does *walk* have the same beginning sound as *water*?
C: Yes.

In this activity, the word *water* was reinforced as a sight word. The children read it both in the story and out of the story context. Furthermore, by being paced through the entire sentence in which *water* occurred, the children had the opportunity to see the value of context as a way of figuring out an unknown word. Assuming that, for the moment at least, the children knew *water* at sight, the teacher used it as an exemplar to teach auditory-visual discrimination for the letter *w*. In this manner, two instructional goals were dealt with simultaneously: teaching sight vocabulary and teaching word-attack skills, i.e., use of context and phonics. Incidental learning which might have occurred included learning the concepts of what a sentence is, how a sentence is marked, and that written words carry meaning.

Sight Vocabulary

As we pointed out previously, the reading of the dictated story in the first lesson provides the initial step in building sight vocabulary. The pattern of the children's language, their memory of what was dictated, and the many repetitions through individual and choral rereading help fix the story in memory. We have seen as many as ten or twelve rereadings immediately following group dictation. With each rereading the children see the teacher point to each word as the word is pronounced. Every child does not remember every word, but every child has the opportunity to learn any or all of the words.

In addition to the group story chart activity there are other occasions when teachers direct the learning of sight vocabulary. On Day 2 of the LEA sequence children are underlining words they know on their individual copies of the dictated story. After a child has drawn lines under all the known words, the teacher checks his knowledge of these words in isolation. This is done by placing a window card over any underlined word. If the child can say the word without using the context, he has learned the word. If he cannot read the word, the teacher draws a wavy line through the underline. The teacher can encourage independence and responsibility for decision making by respecting the child's underlining. Even though the teacher may believe a child knows additional words, only those the child underlines are isolated by the teacher's window card. An underlined and checked story might look like Figure 7.

The same procedure is followed a second time on Day 3. Again, the child draws a line under each known word, this time using a crayon or pencil of a different color. This results in two lines under many words; the second color represents words still recognized on Day 3. Again, the teacher checks the underlined words with a window card, this time checking those underlined in the second color. Any word that the child still knows when the context is obscured by the window card is now considered a sight word. For each sight word the child receives a word card. These word cards represent the tangible product of learning from the dictated story. Word cards are filed alphabetically in the word bank to be used for an assortment of independent follow-up activities.

Using the window card to check knowledge of individual words is one of the best teacher-directed activities for building sight vocabulary. Adequate time should be planned in the daily schedule to allow for this activity to be done regularly. While the teacher checks individuals, good observations can be made of rates of learning, attention to the task, and other behaviors related to a

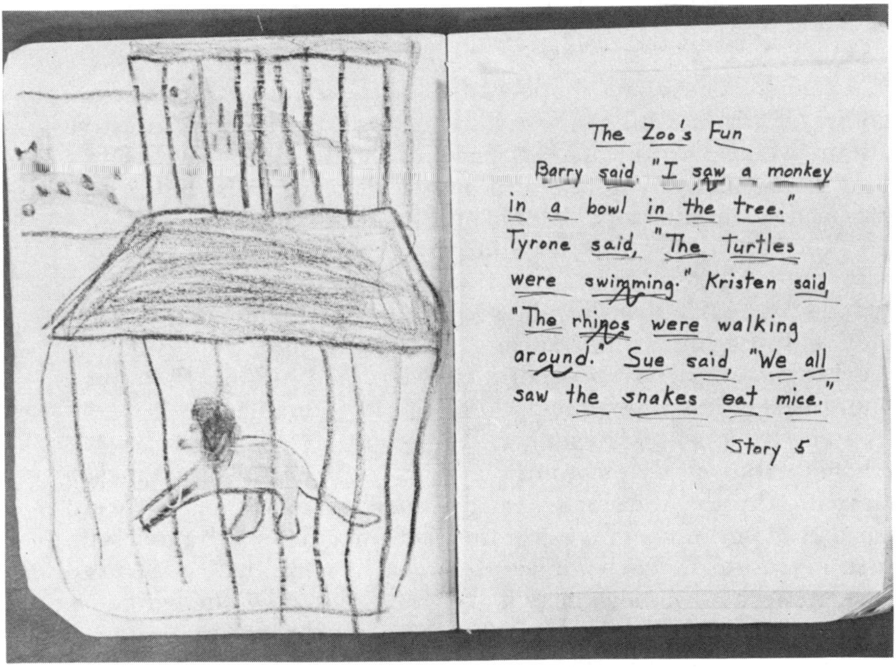

Figure 7: Underlined story

child's ability to retain sight vocabulary. The teacher can learn which children are rapid learners and which are slow, which ones underline too many words that they do not really know well (in their eagerness to please the teacher) and which are very cautious, which ones are steady, attentive learners and which are easily distracted. All these observations can help in planning later activities, evaluating pupil progress, and generally understanding pupils better.

The teacher can include other activities in this session according to the child's fluctuating ability to remember words. Besides checking underlined words with a window card, the teacher may also ask the child to do one of the following activities. These are designed to reinforce sight vocabulary further and to provide additional information about the child's ability to learn and retain sight words.

1. Read the story backwards. This simple change in the task effectively reduces the aid of story context and thus provides a good measure of knowledge of words in isolation.
2. Identify a few words from previous stories when the words are isolated by the window card.
3. Identify a few words from any story when the words are written by the teacher on a piece of scrap paper.

Some teachers have found that using the window card to check known words is a bit time consuming. One particularly effective alternative is to use a word list, made up and duplicated at the same time as the dictated story is duplicated. The word list in Table 7 was made from the story "Elephants" (see page 45).

The random word order eliminates context as an aid to word recognition. Two blanks are included for each word, one for the first day's checking, one for the second. The first checking is equivalent to Underlining I; the second checking to Underlining II. The teacher can simply ask the child to read down the list, then put a check next to the words the child identifies immediately.

This procedure is quick and efficient. It also provides the teacher with a ready record of the words each child learns in each story. In addition, the teacher can use the checked list to make word cards at a later time or may give the list to an aide or volunteer with instructions to make word cards for each word that is checked twice. These advantages may make the use of such checking lists preferable to the use of a window card for some teachers.

It should be noted that the teacher does not decide which dictated story words a child will learn as sight words. Children re-

Table 7
Word List

Elephants

Name _____

Date _____

elephant	___ ___	to	___ ___
he	___ ___	themselves	___ ___
the	___ ___	put	___ ___
is	___ ___	from	___ ___
grown	___ ___	sunburn	___ ___
fifteen	___ ___	getting	___ ___
when	___ ___	water	___ ___
throw	___ ___	on	___ ___
years	___ ___	rice	___ ___
old	___ ___	bananas	___ ___
dirt	___ ___	and	___ ___
keep	___ ___	eat	___ ___

member those words that, because of meaning, configuration, or position in the story, are easiest for them to learn. Usually the easiest words to remember will be the topic word in the story, i.e., *elephants*, the last word in the story, children's names and other highly meaningful nouns, color words, and words that are fun for children to pronounce, such as *squishy, marabou,* or *enormous*.

Teachers sometimes express concern that beginning readers fail to internalize as sight words many high-frequency words such as *and, when, who, but,* or *were*. It is true that these are rarely early sight words. Although children use them when they speak, the words in isolation carry little meaning in and of themselves and thus are not easily remembered. However, these high-frequency words occur over and over again in dictated stories. This repetition in story contexts allows words of such low meaning value to become known as sight words. We have seen some children appear to learn these words all at once. One week they didn't know any of the *wh* words (*when, who, what*, etc.), for instance, and the next week they knew several. This occurred not because of teacher drilling on particular words but rather because of repetition in many stories spaced over many weeks. Teachers may sometimes be tempted to spend considerable time drilling children on these high-frequency, low-meaning words. However, since such drill does not usually result in rapid learning of these words, and is quite dull, besides, it seems more effective to allow the words to be learned in meaningful contexts at the children's own pace.

Word-Attack Skills

In our earlier discussion of the direct teaching that follows recording the dictated story, we emphasized the need to focus on more than just acquisition of a sight vocabulary. Children also need opportunities to learn techniques that will enable them to figure out unknown words they may meet. These techniques, known as word-attack or word-recognition skills, provide the reader with strategies for getting meaning from an unfamiliar word in a sentence. For the beginning reader these skills include use of

1. Context or meaning
2. Phonics or sounding
3. Structural analysis or isolating the root word

Identifying these skills in a list is not meant to imply that they are discrete skills, however. In many instances they are used in combination. For example, if the unknown word is *horse* in the sentence: *The big black horse pulled the wagon*, the reader would probably use the context of the sentence plus the beginning sound of the *h* to guess *horse*. In this instance, then, the strategy would have been to use both context and phonics skills.

If the beginning readers are to develop efficient word-attack strategies it is important that these techniques be taught in combination. Children need many demonstrations, many opportunities to practice unlocking unfamiliar words using a combination of skills. Teacher-directed follow-up activities with the dictated story can provide this kind of learning experience.

Use of Context. In a language-experience story, context clues are particularly useful because the statements in the story have come from the children's own experiences and reflect their own language patterns. Children remember what they have discussed and dictated. They use familiarity with their own language patterns to anticipate words and phrases as they read. Many rereadings of the dictated story further fix the content and language in the children's minds. All these advantages make the use of context clues a natural and relatively easy process for the beginning reader.

Use of context to figure out an unknown word can be taught during the follow-up to the dictated story. This teaching can be conducted while the children are grouped around the story chart, rereading the story. The teacher can point to a word in the story and ask the child, "What is this word?" If the child responds correctly, the teacher can choose another word. When the child does not know a word, the teacher, moving the pointer to the first word in the sentence, can say: "Let's read from the beginning of the sentence." The child reads aloud while the teacher points to each word and pronounces any other words the child does not recognize. (The teacher must not expect the child to figure out every other unknown word in the sentence; only the one unknown word should be the focus of attention.) Usually, when children come to the word in question, they can identify it. (If not, the teacher should pronounce the word.) After finishing the sentence, the teacher should again point to the word, asking, "What's this word?"

After a very few instances of this kind of teacher direction, children will independently follow the same procedure. When confronted with an unknown word, they move to the beginning of the appropriate sentence and start to read. Because it is such a successful strategy, this use of story context as a word-attack skill quickly becomes a much-used procedure for the beginning reader.

Context-clue activities can be of varied difficulty. Fewer clues are needed to recognize intrinsically meaningful words, e.g., key nouns and modifiers, than to identify words with little intrinsic meaning, e.g., most high-frequency words, such as *the, for, to*. Thus, at first, context-clue exercises should focus on nouns, modifiers, and some action verbs, since these words can be more readily identified. As children's sight vocabularies increase and most nouns in the dictated stories are readily remembered, context clues can then be used to identify unknown high-frequency, low-meaning words.

Teachers can also vary context-clue activities according to the number of clues a child needs to recognize a given word. In the following example teacher questions are ordered from those using the least amount of contextual information to those using the greatest amount of contextual information. If a child cannot identify the word, given the first direction, the teacher moves down the list, increasing the amount of context help until the reader can identify the word.

The teacher writes *taste* on the chalkboard.

1. T: What's this word?
2. T: Find the word in the story. What is it?
3. T: (Pointing to the first word in the appropriate sentence.) Let's read the sentence together. (The teacher paces the child through the sentence, pausing at *taste* to see if the child can now identify it.)
4. T: (Pointing to *taste* in the story.) What's this word?
5. T: (Returning to *taste* on the chalkboard.) What's this word?*

If the child could read *taste* in answer to Question 1, the word was a sight word. If the child found the word in the story and immediately responded with *taste*, minimal context clues were used to identify the word. If the child could recognize *taste* after rereading the appropriate sentence with teacher help, maximum context clues were used and the child learned again the value of using context to figure out an unknown word.

This exercise illustrates how skills may frequently be taught in combination. Although the teacher's goal in this instance was to teach the use of context as a word-attack skill, as individual words were identified the children's sight vocabularies were simultaneously being reinforced.

Use of Structural Analysis.   Structural analysis, the ability to divide words into syllables and separate the root and affixes, is a useful word-attack skill. There are many roots, prefixes, and suffixes in the language that give clues to the meaning of many words. Study of many roots, prefixes, and suffixes is usually introduced in the upper grades. Beginning readers are most often taught to recognize common inflectional endings like *s, es, ly, ed,* or *ing* because these endings occur frequently in the language and because once the ending is separated from the root word, the root word is often easily

---

*This series of steps is similar to those outlined in Chapter 3. The difference is that in an immediate follow-up activity the goal is to reinforce sight words learned from the first rereadings of the story, whereas in a skill lesson on using context clues, the goal is to show children how to use context and to give practice in doing so. Thus, in the present activity the amount of contextual information is gradually increased; in the previously described activity, the amount of contextual information is gradually decreased.

recognized. Teaching awareness of roots and common inflectional endings can be accomplished during follow-up activities with the dictated story chart.

Beginning with their initial experience stories, children will use words in their dictation that have common inflectional endings. When a dictated account contains these words, they can be used as exemplars to develop the concepts of root words and endings. The dictated story below includes many words that can be used to develop these concepts.

THE ZOO

We saw the monkeys and elephants.
Zebras are related to horses. The monkey
opened his mouth for peanuts. The zebras
swished their tails. The lion roared. The
tiger roared too.

This story contains examples of *s* to indicate plurality and of *ed* to indicate past tense. Depending on the readiness and abilities of the children, one concept or both could be presented in one lesson. In each instance, however, the same procedures would be used. For the sake of brevity, we will only illustrate the teaching of the plural ending *s*.

First, several rereadings would occur to fix the words and language in the children's minds and to reinforce sight vocabulary. Then the teacher might print *monkeys* on the board and ask some one to read it. This would be followed by printing the word *monkey* and asking someone to read it. The words can be printed in column form to allow easy comparison:

monkeys
monkey

Possible teacher questions might be:

What is different about the way these words look?
Can someone underline the final *s* in *monkeys?*
What is the same in both of these words?
Who can underline the letters that are the same in both words?
(Pointing to *monkeys*.) How many monkeys do we have here?
(Pointing to *monkey*.) How many monkeys do we have here?
How does adding an *s* change the meaning of the word
    monkey?

The teacher can then return to the story and list each example of a word in which the plural was formed by adding *s*. The children should be asked to read each word. The teacher can help them to identify any unfamiliar word by locating and rereading the sentence in which the unknown word occurs. The plural words should also be listed in column form to emphasize the comparison among the words:

    monkeys
    elephants
    zebras
    horses
    peanuts
    tails

Possible teacher questions at this point might be:

    How is the ending the same in each of these words?
    Who can underline the final *s* in each word?
    How many elephants (zebras, horses, etc.) do we have here?

These procedures will call the children's attention to the *s* ending and will help them see the meaning carried by this indication of the plural. At this point, opportunities to reinforce this learning through repeated contrasts of singulars and plurals are needed. First the teacher should write the singular forms of each of the plurals on the board and have the children identify these. These singulars can be written in a column parallel to the "'plurals" column so that contrasts are emphasized. For example:

    monkeys   monkey
    elephants   elephant
    zebras   zebra

Finally, the children should be led to verbalize that the words in the first column mean more than one and that the words in the second column mean only one. Children are usually pleased to find at this point that instead of learning, in this instance, six new words, they can now read twelve new words.

After comparisons are made, the teacher should provide some opportunities for applying the learned skill by having children identify new plural forms, i.e., plurals that have not occurred in the story and are not sight words. "The Zoo" contains two singular forms whose plurals can be used for this purpose: *Lion* and *tiger*. Elsewhere on the board the teacher might write the word *lions* and see if the children can identify it. If the children give no response or respond by saying *lion*, the teacher should say, "This is *lion* (writing *lion* on the board underneath *lions*), now what is *this*?" (Pointing to *lions*). The same procedures would be followed starting with the word *tigers*. For additional practice applying this skill, the teacher could introduce other *s* plurals of singular words the children had learned from previous dictated stories.

Although it is good practice when teaching any word-attack skill to demonstrate that exceptions can occur, when the lesson is an introduction to a concept, discussing exceptions usually is not appropriate. As children become more familiar with a concept, such as forming plurals, and as various forms occur in later dictated stories, the concept can be expanded to include exceptions.

Once this lesson has been completed, the teacher will need to provide other reinforcement activities to give children additional practice in using the newly learned skill. When later dictated stories contain various singular and plural nouns, the teacher can direct lessons similar to the one outlined above. Also, various independent reinforcement activities can be planned.

Lessons like the illustrative *s*-ending lesson can be taught to make children familiar with the various inflectional endings that they most often encounter in their reading. Basal reader teachers' manuals for first-grade materials suggest which endings are appropriate to learn at this level. Such a manual can be consulted to determine which endings to teach. As these common endings occur in children's dictated accounts, appropriate lessons can be planned.

Use of Phonetic Analysis.   Much has already been said and written in the field of reading about phonics instruction. Many professional books deal almost exclusively with the topic; basal reader programs have numerous phonics lessons and exercises from which to choose. We do not intend to outline here a complete phonics program for a beginning reader. Instead, we wish to provide a perspective on the place of phonics in a program using the language-experience approach and some suggestions for teaching and reinforcing those phonics skills individual teachers choose to include in their programs.

Our rationale for phonics instruction includes the following points:

1. Phonetic analysis is only one strategy to use for identifying unfamiliar words. When emphasized more than other strategies, such as context clues, beginning readers may develop an inefficient and ineffective word-attack system; i.e., readers may

"sound out" words when other strategies would be more efficient.

2. Phonetic analysis is a useful word-attack skill only when the unfamiliar word is in the reader's speaking vocabulary. "Sounding out" an aurally familiar word will result in instant identification of the word's meaning. Therefore, phonetic analysis is particularly useful to beginning readers, since easy-to-read materials contain words that are in children's speaking vocabularies. As children grow older, however, and deal with more and more sophisticated reading materials, they increasingly come into contact with many words that are unfamiliar aurally. Even if they "sound out" these words correctly, the words remain essentially unidentified until the meaning is learned. Thus, heavy emphasis on phonics in beginning reading does not guarantee efficient mature readers in later years.

3. Learning phonics is one of the least appealing (and, for some, the most difficult) aspects of a reading program. When more time is spent on phonics than on other reading activities, such as looking at books or reading dictated stories, children can become bored and frustrated with reading. One first grader said it succinctly when he announced, "I like to read books O.K. but I HATE Reading." (*Reading* was, to him, learning to sound out words.)

4. Some children learn phonics more easily than others. If children have difficulty with phonics, the answer is not to give them heavier doses of this instruction. Instead, the wise teacher will help the child make better use of other word-attack skills so that the need for precise use of phonics is reduced.

With these points providing an overall perspective, we will outline a step-by-step procedure for teaching sound-letter relationships based on the use of words from the dictated stories regularly obtained in a language-experience program.

These same steps can be used successfully to teach any sound-letter relationship. Depending on the group's response at different points, more or less time will be needed for each step. For instance, if a group has particular difficulty with auditory discrimination, the teacher will need to spend extra time providing auditory discrimination practice. If a group shows strengths in all areas, the teacher can plan to spend most of the time giving many opportunities to apply the newly learned sound-letter relationships in substitution exercises.

Table 8
Teaching a Sound-Letter Relationship

Steps	Procedure	Dialogue
Start with a known word.	Choose one word from the dictated story that begins with *m*. Print this word on the chalkboard. Ask for volunteers to identify the word. If no one can identify the word, tell the group what it is. Have the group say the word a few times so that, for the purpose of the lesson, the word is known.	Teacher: Here is a word from our story. Who knows what it is? Group: *Monkey*. Teacher: Right. This is *monkey*. Let's say it together. Teacher & Group: *Monkey. Monkey.*
Establish letter name.	Point to the letter *m* in *monkey*. Ask for volunteers to identify the letter name.	Teacher: (Pointing to *m*.) Who knows what letter this is? Group: *M*. Teacher: Good. This is an *m*. We will learn about *m* words today.
Establish auditory discrimination.	Establish auditory discrimination for this beginning sound. Say a number of words that start with the *m* sound and some that do not. In each instance, have the group decide if the word you say starts like *monkey*. Tell the group when they are right, and correct them if they are wrong. Continue with this exercise until the group seems able to make the proper discrimination.	Teacher: I will say a word. Tell me if it starts like *monkey*. *Mother. Mother, monkey.* Do they start with the same sound? Group: Yes. Teacher: Here are some other words. Tell me if they start like *monkey*. *Marble*. Group: Yes. Teacher: *Man. Man, monkey.* Group: Yes. Teacher: *Muffin, Muffin, monkey.* Group: Yes. Teacher: *Car. Car, monkey.*

(Continued overleaf)

Steps	Procedure	Dialogue
	Note: Only the key word is written on the board. Matching words are spoken only.	Group: Yes. Teacher: No, listen again. *Car, monkey.* They sound different at the beginning. Let's try some more.
Establish visual discrimination and list examples.	Have the children find other words in the dictated story that begin with *m*. List these under *monkey* in column form as they are found. Then have the group think of other words that begin like *monkey*. Give them clues to make the task easier if necessary. Continue until there is a list of six or seven *m* words on the board.	Teacher: Look through our story. Find other words that start with *m*. I will write them on the board. (Group finds one or more other words.) Now let's see if we can think of some more words that start like *monkey* to add to our list. What do you drink for breakfast that starts like *monkey*?
Reinforce auditory-visual discrimination.	Have various children underline the first letter of each word listed on the board. Say each word for the group as the *m* is underlined.	Teacher: Joe, put a line under the first sound in *monkey. Monkey* (as Joe underlines *m*). (Other children underline the *m* in other words.)
Establish and reinforce sound-letter association.	Have the group say each word on the list with you.	Teacher: Let's say these words together. Teacher & Group: *Monkey. Mud. Milk. Mother. Mark.* (Etc.) Teacher: Good. All these words start with *m* sound. Let's say them again and listen for the *m* sound.

Steps	Procedure	Dialogue
Apply sound-letter relationship.	Put another word on the board that can be used for beginning-sound substitution. Choose a word that some of the children will probably know, perhaps a word from the current dictated story or previous stories. Substitute *m* for the first letter of this new word and write the resulting word below it. Have the children identify the resulting *m* word. Give help if necessary. Use several words for this substitution exercise, each time establishing the identity of the first word, then substituting *m* for the first letter, writing the resulting *m* word below the original word, and having the group identify it.	Teacher: Here is another word (*can*). Who know what this word is? Group: *Can.* Teacher: Good. (Writing *man* below *can*.) If this is *can*, what is this? Group: (No response.) Teacher: This word (pointing to *man*) starts with the same sound as these words (pointing to the list of *m* words). It starts like *monkey*, etc. *Can*, _____. Group: *Man.* Teacher: Good. Now let's try some more like that.

We have observed that the most successful phonics instruction is accomplished by teachers who plan their own programs rather than relying on the plans and objectives outlined in commercial materials. Nevertheless, some teachers feel more secure if they match their goals for phonics instruction with the goals of a basal reader series. This means making a checklist of the phonics skills identified for instruction in the teacher's manual for the preprimer and primer levels. Although the basal's sequence may not be followed, the teacher will have the assurance that children will receive phonics instruction that will prepare them to read the first books in the basal reading series.

Planning one's own phonics skill program is not as difficult as it might seem at first, and it has the great advantage of allowing considerable flexibility. Teachers are more apt to modify their own programs than to modify a set of lesson plans in commercially published basal series. Unfortunately, when lesson plans appear in print they seem to take on certain intimidating features that may preclude their modification to meet individual student or class needs. We have planned phonics programs with individual teachers and with groups of teachers in K–2 programs and find the following steps work very well.

1. Without consulting any printed materials, list those phonics skills the typical beginning reader probably should learn by the end of Grade 1. For instance,
   consonant sounds—beginning, end, middle
   consonant blends
   consonant digraphs
   The list may be divided into objectives that probably can be mastered by the end of Grade 1 and those that may not seem as important for first graders. For instance, it is questionable whether vowel sounds can or should be mastered thoroughly by the end of Grade 1.
2. Check current professional texts for further ideas on typical first-grade phonics objectives. Add any to the list that were omitted and that seem truly important for the students. Two books that can be useful at this stage are:
   Arthur Heilman, *Phonics in Proper Perspective* (Columbus, Ohio: Charles Merrill, 1976).
   Dolores Durkin, *Teaching Them to Read*, 2nd ed. (Boston: Allyn and Bacon, 1974).
3. Check the basal program(s) used in the school for additional ideas. Do not automatically list any phonics objectives omitted so far; only include those that seem to merit special attention.
4. When the list is complete, categorize the various objectives and prepare some simple checklists for use in keeping records of individual progress.

Comprehension Skills

In the language-experience approach, comprehension is developed during the discussion of the stimulus to help children extend their understanding and attach words to their ideas. Each child is urged to respond to the stimulus in words that describe observations, feelings, and associations; when the stimulus is placed out of sight and the dictation begins, children are verbalizing what they understand and remember. Thus, children are not "taught" comprehension of the story. Comprehension has been inherent in the discussion-dictation process, and there is no need for the teacher to ask comprehension questions or use some comparable "measure" of comprehension.

However, some of the teacher activities designed to teach sight words and word-attack strategies also contain opportunities for developing children's comprehension skills. For instance, children will acquire the concept of what a sentence is if, when teaching use of context as an aid to word recognition, the teacher says, "Start to read at the beginning of the sentence." Children will begin to use the clues of capitalization and punctuation. Sentence sense can also be reinforced by directing children to "Read the sentence that tells . . ."

Sometimes teachers may find it useful to compose a new chart story using children's language patterns and the vocabulary from a dictated account. This teacher story can then be used for a Directed Reading-Thinking Activity (DRTA). The teacher asks the children to predict what they think they will read about and then directs them to read silently to prove or disprove their predictions.* This type of comprehension activity can serve as a bridge to developing comprehension for a variety of printed materials.

Examples of a dictated story and the corresponding teacher story are below. There are a few different, possibly unknown, words in the teacher story. These give children an opportunity to practice their word-attack skills.

SNAKES

Constrictors squeeze the animals that it
eats. The coral snake is dangerous
because it has fangs that have venom.
Horses are scared of snakes. In the
wintertime the snakes stay under a log.

SNAKES (Teacher Story)

We read about coral snakes. Venom
comes out of the coral snakes' fangs. This
venom is dangerous. We read about boa
constrictor snakes, too. They squeeze
baby animals. We are scared of snakes.
We are glad snakes hide in the wintertime.

*More complete explanations of DRTAs can be found in R. G. Stauffer, *Directing the Reading-Thinking Process* (New York: Harper & Row, 1975).

Once children have had experience with a variety of activities of this kind, teachers may choose to introduce other comprehension activities that are similar to the kinds of activities encountered in other reading materials and on standardized tests. For instance, teachers can make up questions that can be answered by rereading the dictated story or by reading a teacher-written story. This procedure is described in chapter 7 and is particularly applicable to dictated stories that contain good amounts of factual information.

Comprehension skills grow as children are exposed to more and varied reading materials. Reading and discussing one another's dictated stories develop comprehension, as does regular reading of materials in the classroom library. Reading and following directions on exercise papers and on other learning materials also reinforce growing comprehension skills. Development of reading comprehension is an integral part of any language-experience program.

INDEPENDENT ACTIVITIES

We have emphasized that the quality and quantity of reinforcement activities significantly affect the success of a language-experience program. This is as true for the children's independent activities as it is for the teacher-directed activities. While the teacher is working with one group of children, the other children in the room should be engaged in meaningful independent work that will continue to build sight vocabulary, word-attack skills, and comprehension. These activities can be either individual or group tasks. Some, like creative writing, require teacher response; others, like word-card games or puzzle assembly, do not. In planning for these activities teachers need to differentiate among children. If activities are to be independent, they must be well within a child's achievement level. Nothing is more frustrating to teacher and child alike than an independent activity which is too difficult. Independent activities also need to be varied. Children need opportunities to engage in tasks that range from practice to problem solving. They need to engage in cooperative tasks and to work alone. They need to examine books, to talk, to write. In sum, independent activities are those that give children many varied opportunities to refine those skills that will contribute to learning to read.

In our observation of many language arts programs, independent skill work usually includes a number of "skill sheets," i.e., workbook pages or exercises that have been duplicated from commercially prepared masters. Although some of these exercises may be appropriate for the children, we have often noted that such published materials do not meet the specific needs of the group to which they are given. More meaningful and useful activities can be planned for children using their experience stories and word-bank cards. Ideas for building various skills by using these basic language-experience materials follow.

As with all independent activities, the ones we recommend here need to be explained and demonstrated to the group before the children can successfully complete the activities on their own. Most of the procedures, however, can be used repeatedly and should, in fact, become standard, frequently used activities in a language-experience classroom. Thus, even though the words and skill focus vary, once children understand how to work at these various tasks, the exercises can be used effectively on a daily basis.

The activities we recommend require children to have much recontact with known words as well as to pay much attention to the basic skills underlying phonetic and structural analysis, i.e., auditory and visual discrimination. We do not, however, find it necessary for children to devote a great deal of time to copying or writing words when they are working on these basic tasks, since the main purpose for assigning these activities is to build *reading* skills. Thus, for those activities involving the use of children's word cards, we recommend that once the word cards have been chosen, categorized, or put in some particular order, the teacher should briefly check the children's work on the spot rather than have the children copy their work and hand it in for later checking. If a volunteer or aide is available, this person can give help with on-the-spot checking. Immediacy is important because word cards have a way of sliding out of place or being brushed to the floor.

In some LEA classrooms, however, the teacher may have very little assistance from other persons and may find it almost impossible to provide immediate response to word-card activities. Such a teacher needs to be resourceful in designing interesting response sheets that require minimal copying and yet relieve the pressure for immediate checking. We have included some examples of activities developed to fill this need (see pages 68–73).

Sight Vocabulary

These activities give children practice in recognizing words they have been learning in their dictated stories.

1. Have children play Concentration using word-bank words. Choose ten or fifteen words that a number of children have in

their word banks. Make two cards for each word. Place all cards face down in three or four rows. Each child takes a turn by turning over two cards and saying the word on each. If the cards match, the child keeps the pair and gets another turn. If the cards don't match, they are returned face down to their original positions and the next child can try for a match. The player with the most pairs at the end is the winner.

2. Have children look for known words in newspapers and magazines. They can cut out known words and paste them on pieces of construction paper to make word posters. For variety, cut the construction paper in unusual shapes, e.g., geometric forms or silhouettes of animals. These posters can be displayed on bulletin boards where the children can read the words to one another at any time.

3. Have the children read current and past experience stories to each other and to visitors to the room.

4. Have children who dictated different group stories try to read each other's experience stories. They can work in pairs to do this; while one child reads, the other can be prepared to help with any unrecognized words.

5. Have children play Go Fish with their word-bank words. Provide a "fishing pole" with a magnet attached. Have the children put paper clips on their word cards and then put the cards in a "pond." When they "catch" a word, they must say it to their partners.

6. Have children work individually and in pairs to categorize words from their word banks. Suggest categories into which some of their words will fit, e.g., names of people, animals, or things to eat. Word cards can simply be lined up in columns for each category.

7. Have children look through trade books and other library table materials to find known words. They can work together or individually. Encourage as much reading as possible besides just looking for words.

8. Have children choose a few "favorite" words from their word banks and draw or cut out pictures to illustrate them.

9. Have children pair up to check each other on their word-bank words. The children can take turns saying words from their own banks to the partner.

10. Have children arrange their word cards in simple sentences. This can be done on desk tops, on the floor, or by using a slotted word-card holder. Children will probably enjoy reading these statements to each other. At first they may need to be

shown how to do this. Take from the word bank four or five words that make a sentence and help the children arrange them in the right order.

Word-Attack Skills

These activities give children practice in using the basic word-attack skills of context clues, phonics, and structural analysis.

1. Have children arrange word-bank cards in groups according to various phonetic or structural elements (whichever are being taught in conjunction with current or past dictated stories). For instance:
   words that begin or end with the same letter
   words that begin or end with the same sound
   words that end with the same element, e.g., -s, -ed, -ing
2. Give children a sheet with two or three drawn pictures (e.g., a kite, a bottle, a fish). Have them find words from their word banks that begin with the same sounds and then group the words under the appropriate picture.
3. Have children arrange a number of word cards in alphabetical order on their desk tops.
4. Give children piles of pictures of various objects. Have them put the pictures in different piles according to beginning sounds or rhyming words. (Pictures can be mounted on small cards and laminated for durability.)
5. Have children make individual picture dictionaries of initial consonant sounds. Pictures can be cut out of magazines or can be drawn by the children.
6. Have children make small posters of pictures and cut-out words to illustrate the beginning sound of each picture.
7. Have children arrange word cards to make compound words. When they have formed a few, have them draw a picture of each.
8. Have children arrange word cards in lists of those to which -ly or -ing can be added. Then give -ly and -ing cards for trial matching.
9. Give children a copy of one of their dictated stories that has been rewritten with some words replaced by blanks. Have children find words in their word banks that can be put in the blanks to make sensible sentences. Words chosen need not be the words that were originally used in the dictated story. (Activities of this kind are often referred to as "cloze" exercises.)

10. Give children simple statements from which one word has been deleted. Have them find one or two word cards that would fit in the incomplete sentences.

Comprehension Skills

These activities give children practice in attending to the meaning of words and sentences.

1. Give children short statements taken from group dictated stories. Have them draw pictures to illustrate what the statements say.
2. Make up a few questions that can be answered from rereading a dictated story. Have children underline the sentences in the story that answer the questions or have them record answers in some way. For instance:

THE PARAKEET

Our parakeet is blue. He sings and chirps. He eats bird food. He sleeps when we put a cloth over his cage. We will try to teach him to talk.

What color is the parakeet?
What does he do when we put a cloth over his cage?
What does he eat?

3. Give children extra copies of previously dictated stories. Have them look for statements pertaining to particular categories. Statements can be cut out and pasted on another sheet of paper with an appropriate heading. Possible categories could include sentences that tell: colors of things; things we eat; what things look like.
4. Construct simple board games for which directions written on cards must be followed to play the game. One direction card, for example, might read "Move to the next red square."
5. Cut an extra copy of a dictated story into sentence strips. Put the cut strips into an envelope labeled with the story name. (Several such story envelopes can be kept in a box.) Have children read the strips and put the story back together in the proper order.

6. After several stories have been dictated, give children a "main idea statement," e.g., "Animals eat different kinds of food." Have them search through several stories to find "details" that go along with the main idea statement. For instance, "The gerbil eats lettuce." "Our rabbit likes carrots." (Extra copies of old stories can be cut up and details pasted onto a sheet with the main idea statement at the top.)

7. Have children work in pairs to play Mystery Sentences. The first child must find a statement in a dictated story and describe the statement to the partner, e.g., "I am thinking of the sentence in Story 4 that tells what we put in cookies." The partner must read the story to find the statement; then it is the partner's turn to think of a mystery sentence.

8. Have children tape their stories. Children in other groups can use these tapes and extra copies of the stories as read-along materials.

9. Have children play Silly Questions. Each child should compose one or two questions using word-bank words, e.g., "Do birds fly?" "Can the gerbil sing?" Composed questions can be given to a partner who must read the questions silently and then answer yes or no.

10. Give children sentence strips from extra copies of dictated stories that lend themselves to dramatization. Have children pick one sentence at a time, read it silently, and act it out to a partner or partners. Viewers must guess what the "actor" is demonstrating.

ACTIVITIES FOR DELAYED TEACHER CHECKING

The following pupil response sheets* are examples of types of independent activities that were individualized for ability groups and designed to follow specific dictated stories. These activities provide for recontact with words in word banks and story books, require a minimum of writing, yet enable a teacher to check them at a convenient time. The activities shown in Figures 8–14 are designed to reinforce sight vocabulary; those in Figures 15–22 are designed to reinforce word-attack skills; those in Figures 23–27 are designed to develop comprehension skills. On some of these activ-

(continued on page 73)

*These pupil response sheets are from an unpublished manuscript by Margaret B. Jones and Peggy Schultz. They are used by permission of the authors.

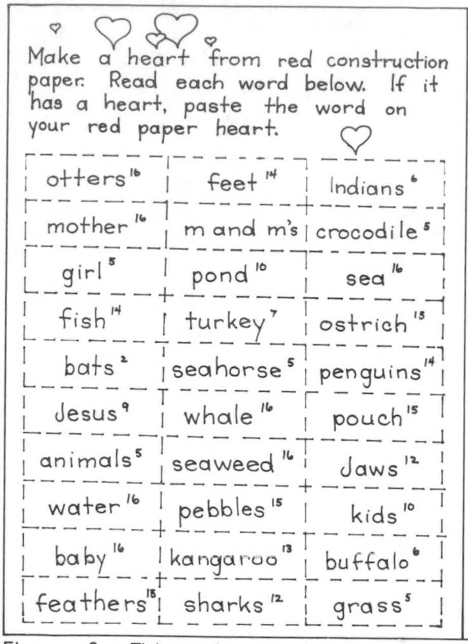

Make a heart from red construction paper. Read each word below. If it has a heart, paste the word on your red paper heart. ♡

otters [16]	feet [14]	Indians [6]
mother [16]	m and m's	crocodile [5]
girl [5]	pond [10]	sea [16]
fish [14]	turkey [7]	ostrich [13]
bats [2]	seahorse [5]	penguins [14]
Jesus [9]	whale [16]	pouch [15]
animals [5]	seaweed [16]	Jaws [12]
water [16]	pebbles [15]	kids [10]
baby [16]	kangaroo [13]	buffalo [6]
feathers [18]	sharks [12]	grass [5]

Figure 8: This cut-and-paste activity in which children categorize living things provides review of sight words.

Mr. Penguin's Rookery

Look in library books for words you can read. Write one word on each stone.

Figure 9: This activity requires recognition of words in various type styles found in library books.

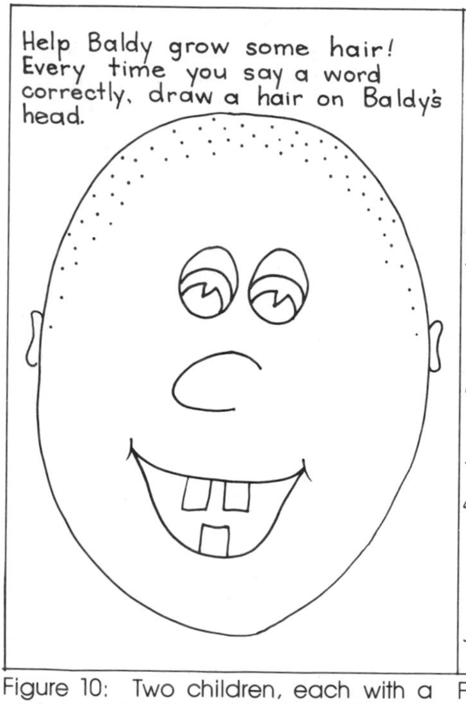

Help Baldy grow some hair! Every time you say a word correctly, draw a hair on Baldy's head.

Figure 10: Two children, each with a picture of Baldy and their word bank, alternately read word cards aloud to each other, drawing a hair on Baldy's head for each word pronounced correctly.

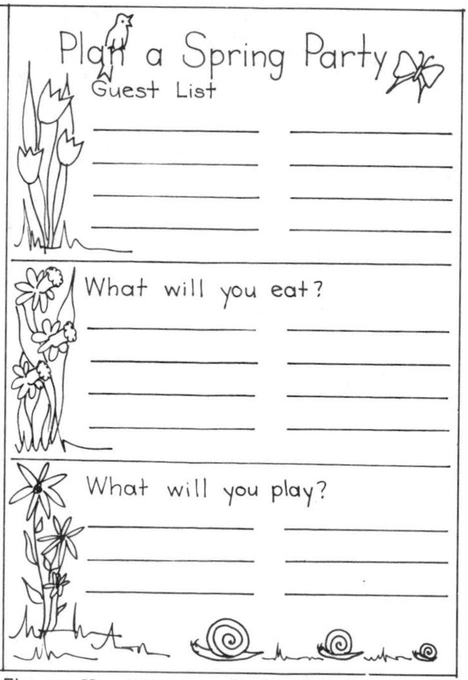

Plan a Spring Party
Guest List
_____
_____
_____
_____

What will you eat?
_____
_____
_____
_____

What will you play?
_____
_____
_____

Figure 11: "Plan a Spring Party" is a thematic activity which requires sorting and listing word cards according to category.

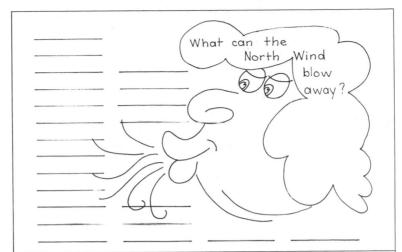

Figure 12: Children can use this sheet to classify word cards in various ways, e.g., words for large or small things, or words with the same beginning or end sound.

Figure 13: The number on each picture clue in this crossword puzzle refers to a numbered story. Children can if necessary locate the appropriate words in their story books.

Figure 14: In this categorizing task, words not recognized at sight may be identified by using context clues In numbered stories.

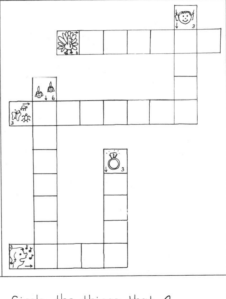

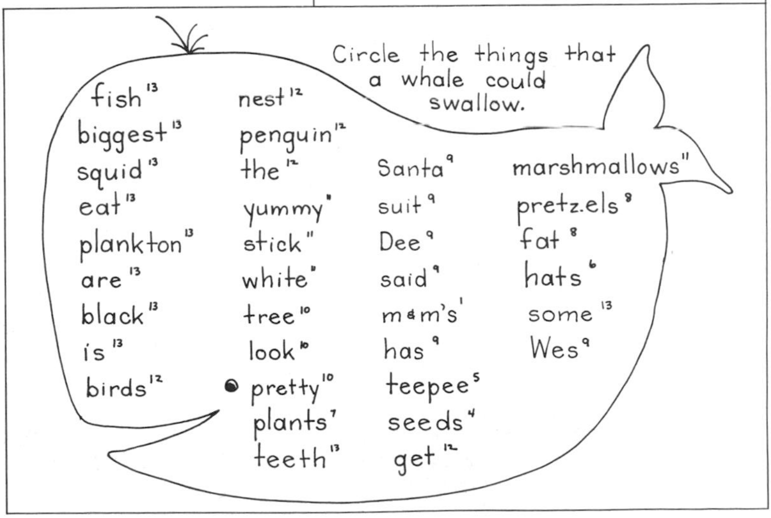

69

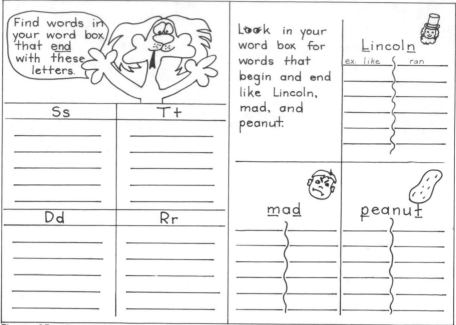

Figure 15: This response sheet is completed by listing words from the word bank which have the final consonants *s, t, d,* or *r*.

Figure 16: Here children are to identify and list word cards that match beginning or ending sounds of the key words.

Look in your word box for words that begin and end like Lincoln, mad, and peanut.

Lincol**n**
ex. like — ran

ma**d**

peanu**t**

Find words in your word box that end with these letters.

Ss	Tt
Dd	Rr

Draw a picture that starts with the same blend.

story[16]	protects[16]
blend[16]	spot[16]
black[15]	sleep[15]
sniff[14]	plankton[13]
blowhole[13]	stones[12]

Find word cards with short vowel sounds.

ă	ĕ	
ĭ	ŏ	ŭ

Figure 17: Children must be able to read the word, identify the initial blend, and produce another word with the same beginning sound.

Figure 18: Children search their word banks for words with short vowel sounds. The words are then recorded in the appropriate box.

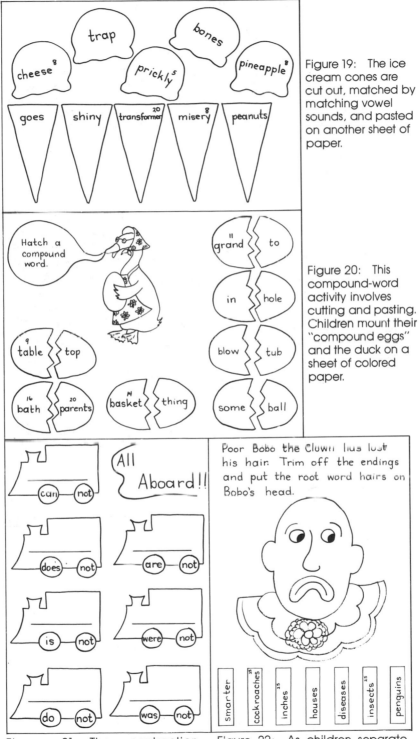

Figure 19: The ice cream cones are cut out, matched by matching vowel sounds, and pasted on another sheet of paper.

Figure 20: This compound-word activity involves cutting and pasting. Children mount their "compound eggs" and the duck on a sheet of colored paper.

Figure 21: The contraction formed by each pair of wheels is written on the engine.

Figure 22: As children separate root words and endings, they also review sight words.

Scrambled Sentences
Story 2

snails	them	out	they	of	
shells	get	rip	their	to	in

their	up	pick	pincher	with
they	food			

eggs	off	have	to	shell	take
their	they	lay	to		

shells	because	their	on	got	them
might	to	they	have	they	get	out

Figure 23: Children cut these sentence strips apart and reassemble the words to match the sentence as it occurred in the dictated story. Sentences are then pasted on colored paper.

Figure 24: This is a teacher-written story that uses words in the children's sight vocabularies. Possible hard words are coded with the number of the story of origin. Children's comprehension is reflected in their illustrations.

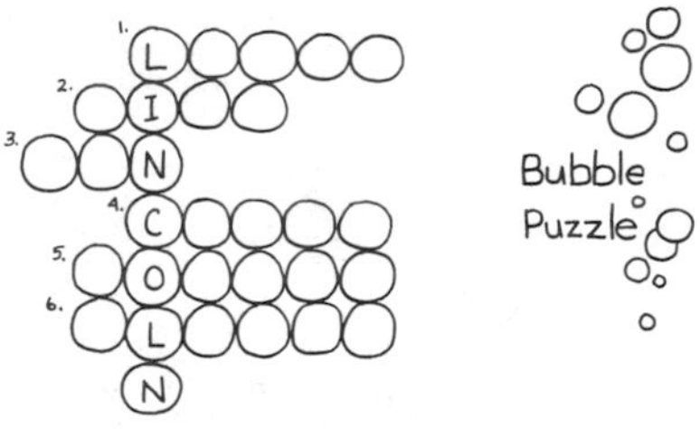

Lisa's Vacation[15]

Lisa[6] was going on vacation. She wears[16] a yellow dress[16] and red necklaces[16] and bracelets[16]. Lisa went to town[5] to get some money[5]. When she got[5] to town, she fell[18] in the mud, but she didn't[18] get hurt[19]. Lisa had spots[20] on the yellow dress.

Draw Lisa.	Draw a yellow dress.
Draw spots on the yellow dress.	Draw Lisa in the mud

Bubble Puzzle

L
I
N
C
O
L
N

1. Lincoln _____ to read books.

2. His mother died when he was _____.

3. He was killed by a _____.

4. Lincoln was born in a _____.

5. Abe's _____ died.

6. Abe set the _____ free.

Figure 25: Children first fill in the blanks in the sentences. (The sentences are based on a dictated story, but with the addition of other sight words.) The word in each blank is then copied in the corresponding row of bubbles.

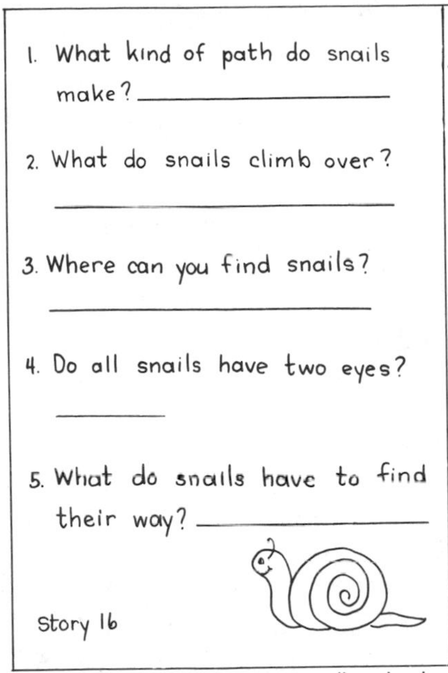

	?? Riddles ???

1. What kind of path do snails make? _____

2. What do snails climb over?

_____

3. Where can you find snails?

_____

4. Do all snails have two eyes?

_____

5. What do snails have to find their way? _____

Story 16

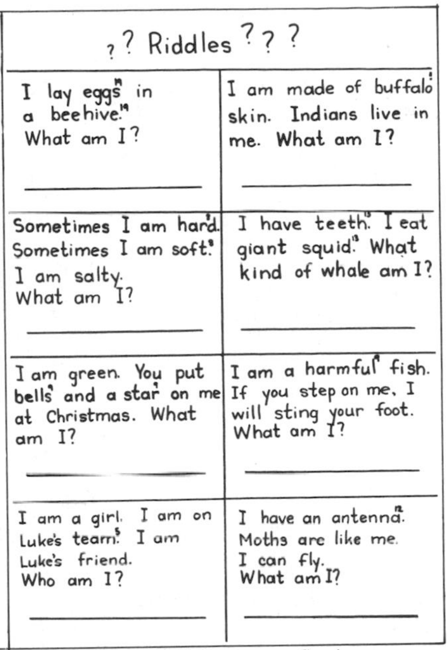

I lay eggs[5] in a beehive.[14] What am I?	I am made of buffalo[6] skin. Indians live in me. What am I?
Sometimes I am hard.[4] Sometimes I am soft.[5] I am salty. What am I?	I have teeth.[6] I eat giant squid.[6] What kind of whale am I?
I am green. You put bells[4] and a star[3] on me at Christmas. What am I?	I am a harmful[6] fish. If you step on me, I will sting your foot. What am I?
I am a girl. I am on Luke's team.[5] I am Luke's friend. Who am I?	I have an antenna.[2] Moths are like me. I can fly. What am I?

Figure 26: Children are directed to write answers to these questions, which are based on a dictated story. (The number of the story is indicated at the bottom of the page.)

Figure 27: Children can find more clues to help in guessing the answers to these riddles if they refer to the story whose number corresponds to that shown in each riddle.

ity sheets the word-bank words are coded with numbers. These numbers correspond to the numbers of the stories in which the words first occurred. For instance, in Figure 14 *fish* comes from Story 13, *nest* comes from Story 12, and so on. If children forget a word, they may return to the story and use story context as a word-recognition clue.

PLANNING FOR SKILL DEVELOPMENT

Each dictated story provides an opportunity for learning new sight words and for review and reinforcement of comprehension and word-attack skills. Each story contains words that can be used as illustrations of various sound-letter associations, and each story contains phrases or sentences that can be used to illustrate other skill elements. Rarely, however, will all the teaching possibilities in a given story be exhausted. Rather, the teacher will select only a few elements of the story to teach those skills that seem appropriate to meet the children's needs at the time. The following examples illustrate lessons that were planned to teach or to review specific word-attack skills. In each instance the decision of which skills to teach or to reinforce was determined by the teacher's judgment of: (1) what the children needed to learn given their present level of reading achievement; and (2) what the story had to offer as good examples of various phonic elements or other skill-related features.

BUTTERFLIES

Butterflies have spotted wings that have green and yellow blood. Butterflies have antennae that can hear and feel for them. Butterflies can see in back of them.

The children who dictated this story could discriminate among beginning and ending consonants and were beginning to discriminate among vowel sounds. The teacher decided to focus on the short vowel sound of the letter *a* and to give practice in discriminating this sound from other vowel sounds. In addition she wanted to emphasize that when the letter *a* occurs in a word it may have the sound of *a* as in *can*. She used the following examples from the story as the basis of the lesson:

can
have
that
and
back
antennae

MOP

She feels soft. She is black and white. You can feel her fur. Mop is a girl dog. She licks your fingers.

This story was dictated by a group of children of rather limited language facility. Within the group were youngsters who were learning to discriminate between capital and small letters, learning the concept of what marks a sentence, and learning to associate the sounds and symbols of initial consonants. To plan appropriate instruction, the teacher surveyed the story for words and sentences that would illustrate these concepts and decided to teach the following: capital and small letters *Ss Yy*; sentences marked with an initial capital letter and a period; auditory and auditory-visual discrimination of the initial consonant *f*, using *feels, feel, fur,* and *fingers* as examples.

WHALES

Whales live in the sea. They have
blowholes. Whales kill fish. Whales swim in
the sea by moving their flukes up and
down. The blue whale is the biggest. The
whales with square heads eat giant
squids.

"Whales" was dictated by a group of children who had mastered beginning and ending consonants and were learning to identify initial blends and digraphs. The teacher used the following words from this story and contrasted them with single-beginning-consonant words from the children's sight vocabularies (i.e., words learned from previous dictated stories).

blowholes	whales
blue	they
flukes	their
swim	

SHARKS

Terry said, "Shark teeth are white and
sharp." Andy said, "Sharks eat fish and
other sharks." Charity said, "A shark can
never float He has to swim." Susan said,
"Some sharks have long tails." Michelle
said, "The sand tiger shark is ten feet
long." Sharon said, "Jaws is a great white
shark."

"Sharks," dictated early in the year, provides many contrasts between single-initial consonants and initial-consonant digraphs. Because the group who dictated this story was not ready for much work with digraphs, the teacher planned auditory-visual discrimination activities to teach and reinforce various beginning single consonant sounds and only introduced one consonant digraph to the group—*sh*. To illustrate the difference between *s* and *sh*, the teacher used the following words from the story:

said	shark
Susan	Sharon
some	sharp
sand	

SKUNKS

Skunks stink. Sometimes they smell bad.
Skunks are black and white. They sleep in
the daytime and hunt at nighttime. They
can see in the moonlight. They have
enemies. The mother saves the babies
when there is something dangerous.

The concept of compound words can be taught any time after
children have acquired the concept of a word, have mastered beginning and ending sounds, and have dictated a story containing
some examples of compound words. Because this story contains
several compound words, it lends itself to teaching the concept.
The teacher of this group chose the following story words for a
compound-word lesson following the dictation of "Skunks":

sometimes	moonlight
daytime	something
nighttime	

In each of these examples of stories and follow-up skill lessons
it is apparent that the teacher planned word-attack skill development according to the needs of the children and the possibilities
within the story. Although there were many skill-development opportunities inherent in each of the stories, the teachers chose only
one or two skills to work with—those that were most needed or
most important at the time for the children who had dictated the
stories. Thus, the teacher may not know, prior to obtaining dictation, exactly which reading skills will be taught in conjunction with
that story; lessons are planned from week to week as the stories are
created in the different groups. However, such a procedure is not
haphazard, for the teacher will have opportunities throughout the
year to teach all the needed skill lessons. The sequencing of skill
lessons may differ from the sequence followed by other teachers,
but the overall goals of developing skilled readers are the same.

SCHEDULING FOR SKILL DEVELOPMENT

Reading in a first-grade classroom is generally scheduled as
part of a morning language arts period. Teachers rather traditionally
place children in several groups according to maturity of skill de-

velopment. Each group meets with the teacher for instruction and then has a block of time for independent activities. However, teachers who are initiating the language-experience approach sometimes feel unsure about planning for that block of time when children work independently. We recommend, as a first step, listing all the many possible independent activities, ranging from easy tasks to more difficult ones. This list should then be divided into two categories: those activities that develop reading skill and those that are related to reading. When planning the time block for independent activity, the teacher can then select some items from each list. A partial listing might look like this:

Reading-skill development:	*Reading-related activity:*
Cut out magazine pictures that have the same beginning sound	Color
	Play with clay
	Assemble puzzles
Reread dictated stories	Listen to tapes/records
Draw pictures to accompany dictated stories	Read along with tapes/records
Underline known words in dictated stories	Look at filmstrips
Do activities using word bank	Practice handwriting (letter formation)
Cut out words and make posters	Play games
	Improvise puppet shows
Write stories	Dress up and improvise plays
Sequence and label pictures	
Read self-selected books	

One way to conceptualize a time and activity schedule is to chart it. The language arts time period can be divided by the number of reading groups to determine the basic schedule of teacher-directed and independent activities. Ideally, skill reinforcement tasks should follow immediately after the teacher-directed activity. This timing allows the independent activity to reinforce the skill just taught. Also, the task of giving directions and getting children started is easier. Once a schedule is established and activities are listed, planning is a matter of continuous recycling. Independent activities of increasing difficulty can be selected to match children's developing reading skills.

The Sample Activity Chart in Table 9 illustrates one day's plan for three groups of children in one LEA classroom.

Table 9
Sample Activity Chart: Monday

Time	Group 1	Group 2	Group 3
9:00	*Teacher-directed* Discuss stimulus Take dictation	*Reading-related* Practice handwriting— Ss and Ll Make a clay horse Listen to story on tape	*Skill-development* Compose three sentences of word cards Complete response sheet on blends Look at books
9:30	*Skill-development* Read favorite dictated story to another child Classify word cards (i.e., according to food, things with wheels, clothing)	*Teacher-directed* Discuss stimulus Take dictation	*Reading-related* Practice handwriting— Ss and Ll Play a bingo game to practice blends
10:00	*Reading-related* Listen to story on tape Make a clay horse Assemble a puzzle	*Skill-development* Read favorite dictated story to another child Classify word cards as in Group 1 Look for known words in library book	*Teacher-directed* Discuss stimulus Take dictation

SUMMARY

Continual reinforcement of sight vocabulary, word-attack skills, and comprehension is a most important part of any reading program. We have emphasized that skill-building activities in a language-experience program should grow from diagnosed needs and should be carefully selected or designed with specific individuals or groups in mind. Commercial materials will be of some use to the LEA teacher; some skill sheets or workbook pages will be useful in meeting specific skill objectives. But teachers should not feel limited by the sequence or type of activities suggested by a particular commercial program. The activities suggested in this chapter represent a sample of teacher-designed lessons and materials that have been used successfully to build basic skills. Good teachers will be able to think of many other interesting activities that will serve the same purpose.

Chapter V

Creative Writing

Most children are delighted with themselves when they learn to read their dictated stories, recognize known words in other contexts, and read stories and books on their own. They are equally pleased and excited when they learn to write their own stories. As soon as children learn the fundamentals of encoding, that is, associating written letters with their sounds, writing and sharing stories becomes a favorite activity. Because writing stories also does much to reinforce and extend developing reading skills, creative writing is a major part of a total language-experience program. In this section, we will present a way to begin creative writing and will suggest appropriate activities for beginning writers. We use the term *creative writing* to refer to any activity in which children express their ideas in written form, whether the resulting account is narrative, expository, or poetic.

PREREQUISITES FOR CREATIVE WRITING

Many aspects of the total language arts program develop the skills that are prerequisites to success in creative writing. Dictation and rereading of experience stories, certain word-bank activities, handwriting lessons, and phonics instruction all build writing readiness in first-grade children.

When children dictate experience stories, they observe the teacher writing their ideas on the story chart. By repeatedly seeing their statements encoded in written form, children learn that writing involves the expression of ideas. Further, as they read one another's dictated accounts, children see that written ideas can be shared with others and so learn to recognize writing as an important mode of communication. Since these activities are a regular part of the language-experience approach, children are continually exposed to the written form of their own thoughts as they learn to read. These experiences help build the children's ideas as to the purpose of written communication in general.

Once children have acquired a number of different word cards in their word banks, they can be encouraged to compose statements by arranging individual words in various patterns. This activity, while reinforcing sight vocabulary, gives children practice in expressing thoughts on their own and helps develop their concept of the specific purpose of written communication. Word-card sentence building is an immediate precursor to creative writing; the more opportunities children have to form sentences in this way, the easier it will be for them to move on to encoding their own ideas in written form. Word-card sentences need not be long and complicated. Simple three- and four-word sentences are typical of children's beginning efforts and are quite adequate for providing practice in this initial stage of composing. The sentences in Figure 28 illustrate the kinds of work that can be expected at this stage, simple arrangements of known words to form meaningful statements.

Handwriting instruction provides children with the ability to form readable letters and words, an obvious prerequisite to creative writing. It is beyond the scope of this book to outline a program for handwriting instruction. We assume that soon after school begins first graders will be given regular handwriting instruction and, throughout the year, will continue to develop handwriting skills. We recognize that children need to have had some such instruction before they can apply their handwriting skills in creative writing tasks. However, we do not equate the handwriting program with the creative writing program. The former aims to help children form clear letters and words; the latter aims at the expression of ideas.

Regular instruction in phonetic analysis skills also provides children with knowledge that is of prime importance in creative writing: sound-letter associations. When the emphasis in creative writing is on the expression of ideas, where it should be, first graders should not be made to feel that they must spell every word correctly. If they are overly conscious of spelling requirements, most children will either limit the words they use in writing to

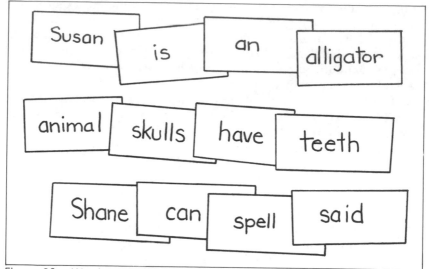

Figure 28:   Word-card sentences

words they know how to spell or else will continually ask for help in spelling every word in their stories. However, if they know that correct spelling is less important than good ideas, they will feel comfortable in spelling as best they can, using their knowledge of letter-sound relationships to sound out words as they write.

These prerequisite skills and attitudes are developed continually in the initial stages of a language-experience program. Since children learn at different rates, however, they will be ready for creative writing at different times during the school year. Some very able children may be introduced to creative writing during the first month of school; others may just be ready to begin at the end of the school year. The average child will usually be able to begin creative writing after three to five months of regular work with the usual language-experience procedures of reading. A child who meets the following criteria will probably be ready to be introduced to creative writing:

1. Has learned most or all single consonant and consonant cluster letter-sound associations
2. Forms most letters and words clearly in handwriting lessons
3. Is able to form statements by arranging word-bank cards

FIRST STEPS

Children should be given as much individual attention as possible as they begin to write. Children should learn that they have important things to say, that other group members do not have to be imitated, and that they do not have to wait for others in order to write a story. To illustrate the basic procedures that can be used to start children writing, we will describe a lesson involving only one child.

First, the teacher should encourage the child to verbalize an idea pertaining to a chosen topic. (We will suggest ways to select a topic and give some ideas for topics later in this chapter.) The child should learn from the beginning to think of an idea and then to write it down. Although this step may seem quite obvious, many children do not know quite how to proceed if simply told to write a story; they need a few moments of guidance in this think-write phase in order to learn how to proceed on their own. The teacher can encourage the statement of ideas by having a brief conversation with the child before the writing begins. A typical conversation might go like this:

> T: You have decided to write a story about your dog. Think of something you would like to say about your dog.
> Jack: I could tell about how he plays.
> T: Fine. That's a good idea. Now what will you say? Tell me how he plays.
> Jack: He runs for his ball when I throw it.
> T: Good. *He runs for his ball when I throw it*. Now, let's write that down.

In this exchange the teacher reminds Jack of the general topic and then encourages him to think of an idea. Of course, the teacher encouraged Jack to state an idea in his own words and did not introduce teacher ideas about what should be said about the dog. The first attempt ("*I could tell about how he plays*") was recognized as a general idea about the dog, so the teacher questioned the child further until he came up with a statement that was specific and would serve as a good beginning to the story. Although this child could have thought of many ideas about his dog, the teacher recognized that only one idea at a time could be written down and so was satisfied when the child stated one thought. Once Jack said "He runs for his ball when I throw it" the teacher repeated the statement and directed his attention to the task of writing the idea in the story. The conversation continues:

> T: The first word you need to write is *he*. Say the word *he* to yourself. What sound do you hear at the beginning?
> Jack: He. He. *H*?
> T: Good. Write that down. (Jack writes *h*.) Now, what is the next sound you hear?

Jack: He. He. *E*?

T: Good. (Jack writes *e*.) Now you have written the first word, *he*. Very good. The next word is *runs*. What sound do you hear at the beginning of runs?

Jack: Runs. *R*.

T: Good. Now, put your finger next to your first word and start the next word on the other side of your finger. (Jack writes *r*. Using his finger as a spacer allows him to leave adequate space between the words.) Now, what is the next sound you hear?

Jack: Runs. Runs. *N*.

T: Fine. (Jack writes *n*.) What is the next sound you hear?

Jack: Runs. *S*.

T: Good. Write it. (Jack writes *s*.) Now you have *He runs. . . .* The next word is *for*. Say it to yourself and see if you can write down what you hear on your own.

After a few moments of this type of guidance and encouragement, Jack's efforts resulted in the following sentence:

He rns fr hs bll wn I thro it.

The teacher read the sentence back to Jack and then had him read it aloud. After praising his efforts, the teacher asked Jack what he would like to say next about his dog, and the same procedures were used. Here is Jack's complete story:

He rns fr hs bll wn I thro it. He is blk and wit. I
lik my dog.

The teacher-pupil exchange and the end product illustrate a number of important points concerning the production of ideas in written form. First, the teacher was careful at all times to be supportive and positive. There was no criticism of Jack's ideas and no attention called to any ill-formed letters or misspelled words. At every step Jack was given encouragement and praise and was made to feel that his story was worthwhile. The teacher did much to encourage a positive attitude toward writing from the beginning by continually placing the emphasis on the expression of ideas rather than on the mechanics of writing and spelling.

Second, we can see that though many of Jack's words are not spelled according to accepted standards, his story is highly readable and evidences excellent command of letter-sound relationships. He appropriately encoded all consonant sounds in his statements and also appropriately encoded some vowel sounds, in particular the long vowel sounds in *he, I, throw, white,* and *like.* Finally, we can see that some words are spelled correctly; these words were probably so well known at sight to Jack that he did not need to sound out to write them; he remembered these words from their constant repetition in various reading activities. We will discuss the diagnostic significance of these observations later. For now, we just note that Jack's story shows marked strengths; Jack's good ear for sounds will allow him to fare well in the future with creative writing.

Our experience has demonstrated that most children need only a few moments of this type of teacher guidance and encouragement before they gain the confidence to move ahead on their own. We recall an instance in which one of us was working with a first grader named Amy, who was writing her first story about her mother. She looked up at her teacher for approval of each letter before she wrote it on her paper. She had written three words in this way when another child came up to the teacher for a moment's help. When Amy realized her helper was not available, she got busy and wrote the rest of her story on her own without waiting for letter-by-letter approval. She was praised thoroughly for her excellent story and was told specifically that the teacher was pleased that she had accomplished so much on her own. Most children catch on to the think-of-the-sound-you-hear strategy after the teacher has guided them through two or three words. Some children may want more feedback and encouragement from the teacher, usually because they want to be sure they are doing the right thing. The teacher should stay with a child until the child seems able to proceed alone and then should encourage the child to go ahead independently.

It is also possible to provide this necessary individual attention in a small group setting. The teacher moves from one child to another giving encouragement and approval and following the same basic procedures with each child in turn. We will illustrate by giving a portion of the conversation and activity that might occur in a group of six, all about to attempt their first stories. The group has been discussing a heavy rainstorm that the whole class had observed that morning. All children have pencils and paper before them.

> T: You all have interesting things to say about the storm. Each of you think of something you want to write in a story. John, do you have an idea?

John: Rain makes puddles.

T: (Moving closer to John.) Good, John. What sound do you hear at the beginning of rain?

John: Rain. Rain. *R*?

T: Good. Write that down. What sound do you hear next?

John: *A*?

T: Fine. And what do you hear next?

John: Rain. *N*.

T: Fine. Put those down. Now you have your first word. What is the next word you will need to write?

John: *Makes*.

T: O.K. See if you can go ahead on your own. Mary, what do you have to say?

Mary: I like the rain.

T: Good idea. You see how John is writing his idea? You can write your idea on your paper. What is your first word?

Mary: *I*.

T: Right. How will you write that?

Mary: That's easy. That's just an *i*.

T: Fine. Now, what is your next word?

Mary: *Like*.

T: And what do you hear at the beginning of like?

Mary: *L*. Do I write *l*?

T: Right. Now you go ahead and see how much you can do on your own. (Moving to Henry.) Henry, what will you say first?

Henry: The clouds are all black.

T: Fine. What do you think you should do first?

Henry: I have to write *the*.

Mary: I just wrote *the*. It starts with a *th*.

T: That's right, Mary. See, Henry? You just think of the sounds you hear in the words. See what you can do now.

John: How do you write *puddles*?

T: What sound do you hear at the beginning of *puddles*, John?

John: *P*.

T: Good. Go ahead. You can sound it out on your own.

Three children have thought of ideas and begun their stories in a few moments' time. The teacher will continue moving around the table to talk with each child, encouraging each to think of an idea and then write each word by thinking of the sequence of sounds in that word. Some children will wait for the teacher's help with each word; others will need only a little encouragement to move ahead independently; some will help one another.

When one group of children seems ready to begin creative writing, the teacher may first work individually with one child in the group. A typical or representative child from the group should be chosen for this trial introductory lesson. Working with this "test case" first will allow the teacher to determine quickly and easily whether or not the group could profit from beginning creative writing. If the individual child performs well, it is likely that others in the group are also ready, and the group can be started. If the child has much difficulty, the teacher should probably wait another few weeks before introducing the group to creative writing.

THE CORRECT-SPELLING ISSUE

When children are encouraged to express their ideas in writing without worrying about correct spelling, they will eagerly write stories and accounts and develop a positive attitude toward writing. The teachers we have worked with recognize this yet are still often tempted to call attention to misspelled words, fearing that children will never learn to spell properly if errors are not noted. Although at first glance our recommended procedure may seem to reinforce poor spelling habits, when evaluated within the broader context of the total language arts program, our recommendations are sensible.

First, we emphasize that the main purpose of creative writing is to encourage children to express their thoughts on paper. Unfortunately, when the mechanics of writing are emphasized in the initial stages, children may develop limited expressive abilities. In a restrictive atmosphere children will come to depend more and more on teacher help, frequently asking how to spell various words they wish to use in their stories. Often their stories will be short, limited to "safe" words, i.e., words they know how to spell. Creative writing may then become a chore rather than a delight. However, if spelling and other mechanical errors are overlooked, children can learn to feel free in expressing their ideas and will usually write more rather than less.

Second, children's unrestricted and uncriticized writing provides the teacher with a constant source of information on the child's developing awareness of letter-sound associations. When children "sound out" words during writing tasks, they are applying phonics skills, and the observant teacher will be able to note how well this knowledge has been learned. To illustrate, we will compare two stories obtained from children in such a writing program.

MY FATHER

My father wrks in a offs. He hs a sekatry.
She tips hs lttrs. My father is vry bse.

Mark

FISH

Fish an fn to kro. Da an ese to kat cr of. Da
hf to be in ratr all da tim. I fd mi fish.

Sally

Mark's story reveals considerable strength in letter-sound correspondence. He has correctly encoded all the consonant sounds in the words he has used and shows some attention to vowel sounds as well. His spelling of the words *office, secretary, types, letters,* and *busy* are all remarkably accurate. Mark's story is representative of stories written by first graders with good phonics skills and should be judged excellent. Sally's story, on the other hand, reveals some difficulties. Her representation of the words *grow (kro), they (da), are (an)* and *water (ratr)* reveal the sounds with which she still seems to have difficulty. She may not be able to discriminate between some sounds auditorially; *g* and *k, d* and *th, w* and *r* may still sound the same to her. Also, there is some indication that she confuses the sequence of sounds in some words; she writes *kat* for *take.* Of course, some of her words show good attention to letter-sound associations—*fun (fn), easy (ese), time (tim),* and *feed (fd)* among others. But, on the whole, Sally's performance is not as good as Mark's. A teacher can use this information to plan additional lessons for Sally in auditory discrimination and other basic phonics skills. Thus, by allowing children to sound out words as they write, the teacher can use creative writing to evaluate progress in learning letter-sound associations and to diagnose strengths and weaknesses in this area.

Finally, though we recommend that first graders not be limited by spelling demands, we do not envision a school's language arts curriculum excluding a good spelling program in later grades. Once children have made good progress in the first-grade language arts program, they can be introduced to a formal spelling program in second grade. Spelling skills that are learned in such a program can then be transferred to the children's daily writing tasks, notably creative writing. Thus, our recommendation to avoid emphasis on correct spelling is limited to children who are beginning to write and who need much positive reinforcement to build positive attitudes toward writing.

We have found that once children are writing frequently and steadily in a relaxed, uncritical atmosphere, they develop on their own the need to spell more accurately. Often, when children misspell words that are in their reading vocabularies, they remark that the words "don't look right" and spontaneously ask if they have written the words correctly or not. Also, when children read each other's stories, the reader often questions the writer as to the identity of some of the words in the story. The need to spell words according to agreed-upon standards is thus demonstrated realistically and directly to the writer. At these times the teacher can show the child the correct spelling of the words in question and can praise the child's attentiveness to his or her own work. An error recognized by a child is not the same psychologically as an error pointed out by a teacher. When given the freedom to make errors in writing, children will eventually recognize many of their own mistakes and will often, on their own initiative, seek to be more accurate. This attitude should, of course, be reinforced, since it is much more appropriate than a drive for spelling accuracy motivated by a fear of being criticized.

When children do recognize on their own the need to spell more accurately, the teacher should certainly help them to spell better. A number of spelling aids can be used independently by children who want to increase their accuracy. For instance, the teacher can suggest that children refer to their word banks for words they are using in their stories. A child can find a word and copy the letter order from the word-bank card. Picture dictionaries can be used to find some words as well. Finally, in some instances, the teacher may write the word for the child on a piece of scrap paper; this model can then be copied in the child's story. These aids should be suggested and used only when children take the initiative to improve their own spelling. In no case should a child be overly concerned with correct spelling, since such compulsion will usually limit the expression of ideas and turn creative writing time into a laborious word hunt.

We have found that in a relaxed, supportive environment marked by the freedom to make mistakes, children learn positive attitudes toward written expression and learn to write freely. Eventually children begin to note errors in the mechanics of their writing and then can learn to be more attentive to accuracy. While they are learning to write, their spelling errors can provide the teacher with good information as to their growing skill at making associations between letters and sounds. Thus, we strongly urge that teachers learn tolerance for children's spelling errors in the interest of reaching the long-term goal—children who like to write.

ASSESSING PROGRESS IN CREATIVE WRITING

A sampling of a child's writing collected over a period of time provides a good measure not only of ability to express ideas but also of facility with letter-sound relationships and of handwriting skill. Teachers can see growth over time by keeping files of creative writing stories for several months. Such files can be helpful when evaluating progress through the year. For instance, the stories shown in Figures 29–32 (and also translated) illustrate one child's progress in creative writing during a first-grade year.

In Story 1, written in November, Ann demonstrates considerable phonics knowledge. She accurately records consonant sounds that she hears and has even recorded the sound of the consonant digraph *th*. Apparently she is aware that vowels belong in the middle of words, although she does not yet know the correspondence of sound and letter. She does show, however, by her spelling of *house* that she has learned that spelling of words is usually consistent. Note that in a story of thirteen running words, Ann knows the standard spelling of eight. Ann's handwriting is also revealing. Her tilted letters and mixture of capital and lower-case letters indicate a beginning grasp of manuscript printing. The size of her final periods suggests that this may be a new and, for her, very important concept.

Ann's second story sample was written in late January. This story contains twenty-six running words, of which all but four are correctly spelled. Ann's spelling of *white* and *died* show a growing although inconsistent awareness of vowel letter-sound relationships. By spelling *died* with a final *e*, she demonstrates that she knows vowels often have their long sound when the word ends with a silent *e*. Although Ann still confuses capital and lower-case letters, her handwriting here is much more regular than in the preceding sample. Her reversal of the final *g* but not the initial *g* suggests developing control over letter formation.

Ann's March story is not only longer than the preceding stories; it is also titled. Her handwriting skill has increased greatly, both in letter formation and in spacing. Also the high-frequency words such as *they*, *are*, and *can* are correctly spelled. Phonetic spelling of other words shows clearly which sounds Ann hears. Consonant

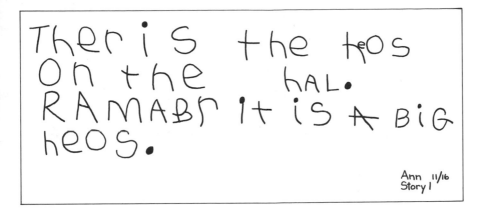

Figure 29: Story 1

There Is the house
on the hill.
Remember it is a big
house.

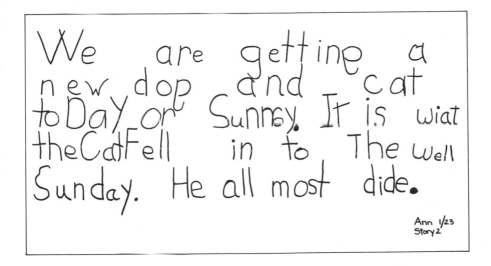

Figure 30: Story 2

We are getting a
new dog and cat
today or Sunday. It is white.
The cat fell into the well
Sunday. He almost died.

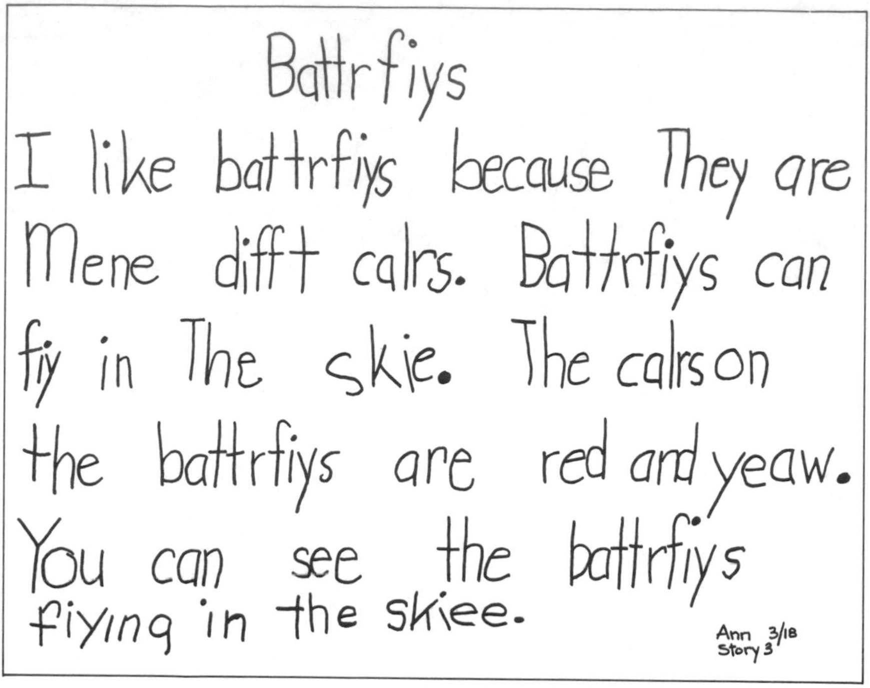

Battrfiys

I like battrfiys because They are
Mene difft calrs. Battrfiys can
fiy in The skie. The calrs on
the battrfiys are red and yeaw.
You can see the battrfiys
fiying in the skiee.

Ann 3/18
Story 3

Figure 31: Story 3

BUTTERFLIES

I like butterflies because they are
many different colors. Butterflies can
fly in the sky. The colors on
the butterflies are red and yellow.
You can see the butterflies
flying in the sky.

sounds are fairly well established, as are the vowel sounds of *e* and
i. The vowel sounds of *o* and *u* are not yet reflected in Ann's writing. It is interesting to observe her consistent omission of the *l* in
both *fly* and *butterflies*. Nevertheless, she maintains a consistent
spelling pattern for these words.

The fourth sample is a story that was written toward the end of
Ann's first-grade year. It shows her increasing ability to convey a
message. Without the constraint of accurate spelling, she records
her oral language in a natural and unstilted manner. Nevertheless,
of seventy-seven running words, sixty-five maintain conventional
spelling. The spelling of the remaining words reflects Ann's ability
to sound out words. In the interval between the writing of Story 3
and Story 4, she has learned the vowel sound of the *u* and is gaining

My Mother

Me and My Mothre We did a pusl.
it was fun. We did it in One day
there are three lost. My Daddy
Can't put a pusl to gether. My
Daddy Said We are the Best
pusling girls. We wer Very happy.
And Went to see are Cusin he is
a baby. I Culdent go in decause
I Was Kallfing and may be I wud
give the baby a Calld. thats wiye
I didt see The baby.

Ann 5/21
Story 4

Figure 32: Story 4

MY MOTHER

Me and my mother we did a puzzle.
It was fun. We did it in one day.
There are three lost. My daddy
can't put a puzzle together. My
daddy said we are the best
puzzling girls. We were very happy.
And went to see our cousin he is
a baby. I couldn't go in because
I was coughing and maybe I would
give the baby a cold. That's why
I didn't see the baby.

control over the *o* sound. Ann is apparently also aware of the inflectional endings of *end* and *ing*. Because of Ann's inconsistency of punctuation and letter formation, we suspect that her interest has shifted from these aspects of writing to more concern with the telling of a story.

These four stories give a graphic picture of one child's progress in both writing and knowledge of phonics. They readily demonstrate how useful children's creative writing can be in evaluating instructional progress. A teacher can literally see which letter-sound associations the child is making while reading.

One teacher with whom we worked made a practice of saving all the children's stories for a month. Each child's stories were kept in a folder labeled with the child's name. At the end of each month, the stories were reviewed and the most representative one retained in the folder. The rest of the stories were stapled together for the child to take home. At the close of the school year and after a summary evaluation had been made, the folder of stories was returned to the child. This teacher found the folders of creative writing samples of inestimable value when discussing children's progress with parents.

Teachers sometimes feel that once creative writing is underway in a classroom with children writing on a regular basis the need for story dictation ceases. We have heard the argument that if children's writing were "cleaned up," i.e., spelling and punctuation corrected, these stories could then be used for reading instruction. We urge teachers not to follow this practice. While creative writing supports and supplements the language-experience approach, it is not a substitute for dictation.

Dictated stories reflect children's oral language transcribed by the teacher. In this setting children learn to use language naturally and fluently rather than laboring to write one word at a time, trying to keep a complete thought in mind until it is written down. Although it is exciting to see what beginning writers can produce, rarely would either the quality or the quantity of children's written language equal their dictated language. Compare, for instance, the following examples of children's writing with the story dictated by their group during the same week. Even if spelling and punctuation were corrected, the creative writing lacks the variety of vocabulary and sentence structure seen in the dictated account.

Thus, written stories allow children to express ideas in a unique form and to enjoy the process of writing, while dictated stories continue to build oral expression and composition skills. Both writing and dictating contribute to children's growing mastery of language.

CREATIVE WRITING

The lady was olde. The popits wore funny. P.O. wos vary! funny. Pkom wos too. The man had brone hair.

Carol

I kaiot a thirtin ieh baes. Kaiot a big fihe. Daddy pot it in the bokit. Tuor aur skoles on a fihe.

Andy

DICTATED STORY

Lincoln was born in a log cabin and he grew up tall real fast. He had to walk a long way just to get a book. He sat by the fireplace and read all night long. When he got big, he became president.

SUGGESTED TOPICS FOR CREATIVE WRITING

Most children do not have a store of ideas to use for creative writing topics. If simply told to write a story, they will most likely be unable to think of anything to write about. Thus, teachers must suggest ideas to help children decide which topic to select. There are no hard and fast rules to follow when choosing creative writing topics. In general, whatever children are interested in will suggest the subject matter for their stories. Many teachers' guidebooks and manuals give ideas for creative writing topics; teachers may suggest these to children or may suggest topics relating to children's daily activities. We will outline a number of different ways to suggest topics for creative writing, recognizing that each has its usefulness and that no one way will necessarily work at all times for all children.

Special Events

Whenever something out of the ordinary occurs in the school day, it can be used to stimulate creative writing. Classroom visitors, for instance, often provide excellent stimuli for stories. A local police officer or firefighter, a parent demonstrating an art lesson, a principal giving a talk to the class, or a public librarian paying a visit can all spark interest and be described in the stories of that day. Special classroom activities can also be used to motivate good stories: planning a Halloween party, decorating a group present, taking a field trip to a local point of interest. Unusual weather phenomena such as a heavy rain or the first snow can also stimulate ideas. Whenever children show interest in an event and are eager to talk about it, the teacher can encourage discussion and then suggest the good ideas be recorded on paper.

Brainstorming

To provide topics for a few weeks or a month at a time, the teacher might engage children in a brainstorming session. The initial question could be, "If you could write about anything you wanted to write about, what would you choose?" Children will usually respond to such a question by suggesting many different ideas, which can be listed on the board or on chart paper for future reference. One class we visited had come up with the following list of titles:

Dogs	Airplanes	My Father's Boat
Cats	Train Rides	Catching Fish
My Fish	My Apartment House	Policemen
My Mother	Elevators	CB Radios
My Father	The Bionic Man	The Zoo
My Teacher	The Bionic Woman	School

When children had difficulty thinking of ideas, the teacher would ask individual children questions such as: What do you like to do? What do you watch on television? Where did you go yesterday after school? What pet do you have? and so on to stimulate further ideas. The class topic list can be posted for a few weeks. Whenever children write a story, the teacher can review the list with them, and some children will get an idea for the day.

Fanciful Topics

Sometimes children enjoy making up fanciful stories or imagining themselves in unusual or remarkable circumstances. A number of ideas lend themselves well to this type of creative writing, for instance:

If I Had One Million Dollars
If I Were the Teacher (Principal, etc.)
The Green Monster
I Am the Bionic Man (Woman)
The Day My Dog Talked to Me

Topics like these can stimulate divergent, imaginative thought and often result in delightful stories. We emphasize, however, that imaginative stories like these are no more "creative" than stories that describe everyday objects and people. Whatever a child chooses to write about is the result of some creative thought, whether the ideas are farfetched or down to earth.

Standby Topics

Many topics can stimulate stories when it seems there is nothing special to write about. Teachers and children may well run out of good ideas from time to time, and some standard suggestions can be used at these times. A few standby suggestions we have used successfully in the past include:

Describe everything you see in the classroom.
Write a story about the person sitting next to you.
Look out the window and write about what you see.
Describe your shoes (shirt, dress, etc.)
Write about what you will do when you go home today.

PREWRITING PREPARATIONS

No matter which topics are suggested or chosen for creative writing, some discussion prior to writing is needed to stimulate thinking and help children decide what to say. As many children as possible should be encouraged to offer comments during a prewriting discussion. The more that is said during the discussion, the more words and ideas children will have to use in their stories. To illustrate, we will give a portion of a good prewriting discussion we once observed in a first-grade classroom.

T: Many of you have been talking about the aquarium we brought into class yesterday. Some of you might like to write stories today about our aquarium. Let's think of what you could write about in your stories. Who has some ideas? (Many hands go up.) Ralph, what's your idea?

Ralph: It's got all those plants and rocks for the fish to swim around in and we get to feed the fish.

T: Those are good ideas. Sara?

Sara: We can tell how cold the water is from the thermometer.

T: Sam?

Sam: Can we get more fish?

T: We might be able to. Do you remember what kinds we have already?

Sam: There are some goldfish there and some other kind with stripes.

T: Martha?

Martha: The aquarium has lots of rocks in the bottom like the ocean.

The teacher called on other children to offer ideas as well. All the children looked at the aquarium more closely and the different ideas that were brought out gave many children ideas of things to say in their stories. The teacher encouraged comments but avoided telling the children what to say in particular. When many children had given ideas, the teacher summarized the discussion:

> You have many good ideas to put in stories. You could tell about what kinds of fish we have and what other things like rocks and plants we have in there too. You could write about how we feed the fish and how we watch the thermometer to see how cold the water is. You could write about why you like the aquarium and what else you might put in it. Everyone has something good to say. Let's get busy and write stories.

This kind of stimulation will usually encourage many children to begin stories eagerly since they will have become interested in the topic and will have thought of something to say.

We have found that some children do not begin stories as easily as others, however. Even after a lively discussion of one or two suggested topics, there may be some children who can't seem to get started. The teacher will need to check with these children individually to find out what the problem is. It may be that despite a good prewriting discussion a few children still haven't thought of an idea and need additional conversation and encouragement from the teacher. Others may be reluctant because they are not really interested in the suggested topic(s) and don't want to write anything. For these children alternative choices can be suggested by the teacher and discussed with each child.

ACTIVITIES RELATED TO CREATIVE WRITING

Certain nonwriting activities can make creative writing even more enjoyable and can add to children's appreciation of writing as a form of communication. These activities include illustrating stories and sharing stories.

Illustrating Stories

A natural follow-up to creative writing is to draw an illustration to accompany the story. If regular first-grade composition paper is used for writing, the illustration can be placed at the top of the page. Regular drawing paper might also be used for the illustration, and the story can be fastened to this extra sheet. Children usually enjoy illustrating their stories, often including more details than they mention in the stories themselves. The stories and illustrations can then be displayed in the classroom for all to enjoy.

There are also times when children's illustrations can be used as the stimulus for creative writing. Individuals can draw pictures of favorite animals or people, imaginative characters, or various scenes and objects; groups can also prepare murals or posters on a number of different topics. These can all be used to stimulate the writing of stories to accompany the drawings.

Sharing Stories

Children should always be encouraged to share their creative writing with one another. A few minutes can be set aside each day for individuals to read one of their stories to the class and show any accompanying illustrations. This activity helps to demonstrate the communicative function of writing and further stimulates interest in writing, since having a story to share soon becomes a goal all children want to reach. Children can of course also be encouraged to read their stories to one another in a less formal way in small groups or pairs whenever extra time is available.

Story sharing can result in general improvement of the stories that are written in a class. As children hear one another's ideas, they may get ideas to use in their own stories. When a child writes an imaginative story, others may be motivated to use their imaginations. If one child describes a pet or a best friend, a number of pet or best-friend stories will often be written the next day. And of course children will often use vocabulary and sentence structures that they hear used frequently in their classmates' stories.

Less direct ways of sharing stories should also be arranged in the class. Children's creative writing should be posted frequently for all to observe and read. A special display area can be set up for this purpose. Stories can be tacked on bulletin boards or hung from a clothesline with clothespins. Stories on the same topic can be grouped together or stories from one group can be displayed in the same place. Stories might even be "bound" into booklets and placed on the library table; or children might like to copy their stories into blank teacher-prepared books (see Appendix A for directions on making books) which can then be available for all to read. An "Author of the Week" display can also be set up, allowing one child a week to be recognized for his work.

SUMMARY

Creative writing plays an important part in a language-experience program. Writing activities provide good diagnostic information to teachers and allow children to expand their understanding of and control over language. In the first stages, in first grade, the emphasis should be placed on the pleasure of expressing ideas and describing events rather than on the mechanics of spelling and punctuation. With regular encouragement to write, children will perceive writing as enjoyable and will gradually improve their skills.

Creative writing should not, however, be considered a substitute for dictating stories. Once children begin to write, they should still be given regular opportunities to dictate stories for the purpose of continuing to develop reading skills. Oral vocabularies and sentence structures will still be more advanced than written vocabularies and sentence structures; regular dictation continues to help children use oral language more effectively. Also, group dictation, especially, continues to give children the chance to hear and learn from the ideas and expressions of their peers. Thus, writing should not replace dictation but rather should supplement and enhance the well-established reading activities in a language-experience program.

Chapter VI

Variations
on
Basic Procedures

Although we have been rather explicit about the language-experience procedures to use in a developmental reading program, there are situations where variations of these basic procedures are appropriate. This chapter will include discussions of the following variations:

Individually dictated stories
Language-experience integrated with content areas
The use of language-experience in kindergarten
Language-experience as a supplement to a basal reader program
Language-experience for remedial instruction

INDIVIDUALLY DICTATED STORIES

In earlier chapters we described language-experience procedures as they relate to the group-dictated story, that is, the dictated story composed of contributions from a number of children. There are times, however, when dictated stories can be obtained from individual children. Most often, individual stories are included in children's programs after they have spent some time contributing to group stories, have well-established word banks, and are accustomed to the basic procedures. This section will present a way to achieve this completely individualized variation.

Procedures

Essentially the same procedures are used to obtain an individually dictated story that are used for obtaining group stories. That is, the teacher and child briefly discuss a stimulus or topic for dictation; the child states ideas, and the teacher records the statements for use as the basic reading material. The story is then reread a number of times with teacher help; known words are underlined, and word cards are made for inclusion in the child's word bank. Individual stories can be printed directly in the child's story book at the time of dictation, or a typed copy can be prepared to be fastened in the story book.

There are some minor differences between procedures for obtaining group and individual stories. First, since the single child is the only contributor to an individual story, his or her name is not used in the body of the story. That is, the story is not begun with the phrase *Jack said* or *Sally said*. Second, the length of the story is determined solely by how much the child has to say and how long a story the child can handle with ease. Thus, there is no "average length" for an individual story. Some may be only a sentence or two long, others may extend for a page or more. After obtaining two or three individual stories from a child, the teacher will be able to judge a suitable length for that child.

If a group of children are all going to dictate individual stories, a teacher may present the same stimulus to the group for the usual observation/discussion prior to dictation. Then each child in turn can sit with the teacher to dictate an account. Or, the teacher may not provide the stimulus and may instead say to each child, "What would you like to dictate about today?" This last procedure is especially workable when children have had a number of individual dictation sessions and also have many things to say about many topics.

Advantages of Individual Stories

There are many situations in which individual dictated stories are preferable to the usual group-dictated stories. First, a round of individual stories from one group can provide good variety in the overall program. Individual stories can serve as a change-of-pace strategy, and thus might be used periodically throughout the year for children who otherwise spend their time working with group-dictated stories. Every two or three weeks the teacher can dispense with the usual group story and have the children devote a week's time to work on their own individual stories. Certainly the undivided session is a positive feature; each child will feel special, valued for his unique personality and ideas at this time.

Also, individual stories can be quite useful for providing challenge to the rapid learners who master group-dictated stories quickly and easily. Such very able youngsters often have many interests and ideas that cannot all be included in a group story. Also, the advanced child usually has a well-developed speaking vocabulary and uses relatively mature sentence structure. An individual story allows such children freer reign for their unique and advanced expressive abilities. For the very able child, use of individual stories extends the challenge of reading and allows maximum opportunity for learning new words and skills.

Conversely, individually dictated stories may be useful in a different way for the child who makes slower progress. An individually dictated story can be taken with that child's particular needs and interests in mind. For instance, the teacher can take care to limit the story to one or two statements to reduce the demands of dealing with a whole page of words. Also, an individual story based on a child's strong personal interest can increase motivation for learning to read the story. This point is especially important to keep in mind for those children who show little interest in the usual stimuli used for dictation or who become increasingly frustrated with the task of reading. Finally, the child will only need to read those statements that reflect his own language patterns and background of experience. For some children, even trying to read classmates' language may be difficult, especially if the individual's language differs significantly from that of the others in the class. For instance, for children who speak non-Standard English or who are bilingual, individually dictated stories can be tailored to meet their particular language patterns and growing Standard English awareness in a way no other material can.*

Individual stories can also serve an evaluative function. Periodically, perhaps every six weeks, the teacher can substitute individualized dictation for the group story. Evidence of growth can be charted and compared from one occasion of individualized

---

*The usefulness of LEA for bilingual children has been described well in Carol Dixon, "Teaching Strategies for the Mexican-American Child," *The Reading Teacher* 30 (November 1976): 141–145.

dictation to the next. Observations can include attention to a child's ability to focus on one topic, the length of the story, the number of different words, the complexity of sentences. In addition the teacher can record a child's ability to reread the story and the number of sight words learned. These observations can provide a useful measure for both teacher evaluation of progress and for reporting to parents. (See Table 10 for an example of such an individual record sheet.)

Difficulties with Individual Stories

Although there are many advantages to obtaining individually dictated stories in an LEA classroom, there can be some difficulties with such a highly individualized program. Getting individual stories from a class of twenty-five or thirty first graders takes time and extra attention to organization to make things go smoothly. We can offer some suggestions for coping with the problem of teacher-time management in this situation. The most obvious, of course, is for either an aide or a volunteer to be enlisted to record individual dictation. This solution gives children the advantages of being able to dictate individual stories while freeing the teacher to spend time with small groups in direct instruction. However, in the absence of another person to record dictation, a teacher will probably find that short periods of time, scattered throughout a week, will have to be used for recording individual stories. Generally a teacher needs to plan for about ten or fifteen minutes for each individual dictation. This is possible if dictation is slotted into various times during a day and scheduled daily until each child has dictated. A dictating/recording schedule of this sort means, however, that children will not all have a new story on the same day. To assure that each child dictates at least once a week, a checklist can be maintained. If dictated accounts are recorded directly into story books, the duplicating process can be eliminated. Many teachers find that placing carbon paper and a blank sheet of paper under the page as they record dictation provides a copy for easy reference when planning teacher-directed and independent skill-development activities. Planning for group instruction is much easier if one can refer to the collected group of stories. As an additional aid in planning, some teachers find it helpful to borrow children's word banks periodically and list each child's sight words. Even though children have different stories and some variation in sight vocabulary, reading skills can be developed more efficiently by using group instruction with those sight words children do have in common.

Table 10

Chart of Individualized Story Record

Name	Date	Topic	Words	Different words	Complexity	Rereading	Word cards	Comments
Suzy Bishop	10/20	Caterpillars	47	21	1 compound sentence 8 modifiers	Good	18	Good focus to story
	12/2	Baby Brother	57	29	6 modifiers	Good	24	Might have been longer, but S. wanted to work on an art activity
	2/8	Snowman	83	34	1 compound sentence 1 complex sentence 5 modifiers	Good	33	Reading many trade books; will try her in primer

In addition to the challenge of scheduling for individualized dictation, there is the challenge of providing enough practice opportunities for rereading and "learning" the story. The group activity of rereading the chart story is not available. However, children can reread their stories to their peers either with partners or in small groups. What happens when a word or phrase is forgotten? Usually there is someone in the room who can help identify a puzzling forgotten word. Children quickly learn who those persons are and go for help. A spirit of cooperation is therefore frequently a happy by-product of this procedure. Children can also gain rereading practice by reading into a tape recorder, listening, and rereading until satisfied with the performance. Teacher-directed group activities can include rereading sentences that contain a particular content word such as *peacock*, or searching for and rereading sentences that contain word elements such as *ing* words or words with the vowel sound of the "long *a*." One teacher we know makes a practice of expecting that every visitor to her classroom will listen to at least one child read a dictated story before that person can state the reason for the visit. Her students greet a knock at the door with a flurry of story book opening. They read to the janitor, the principal, the messenger from the classroom next door, the visiting parent. This opportunity to read to visitors seems to have high prestige value and provides motivation for mastery of individual stories.

Teachers need to view the individually dictated story as one option when using the language-experience approach. We recognize the potential management problems but believe that there are situations when the benefits of individualized dictation justify the additional teacher effort.

LANGUAGE-EXPERIENCE INTEGRATED WITH CONTENT AREAS

In many schools reading is seen as a separate content area; "reading" is taught at a certain time of the day, usually in the morning, and materials are designated as "reading" materials as opposed to "science," "social studies," or "mathematics" materials. However, most teachers recognize that reading skills are used in all curriculum areas and that there is no real justification for thinking of or teaching reading as a separate subject. Basal reader series also recognize to some extent that reading skills are applied in many subjects; published series include many types of selections (nonfiction, fiction, poetry) to give children practice in dealing with varied reading demands. Some series are even organized around certain content areas, such as science or social studies. However, in most classrooms, even with well-designed basal materials and good teacher intentions, there is minimal integration of the language arts program with other parts of the curriculum. Reading is taught in a discrete block of time as a separate subject.

One of the major strengths of the language-experience approach is that, of all available reading programs, it is the program that can be integrated most easily and effectively with other curriculum areas. In a language-experience classroom the teaching of reading need not be limited to a portion of time during the "language arts" period. Reading, other language arts, social studies, and science can be taught in a well-integrated overall program. In this section we will suggest how this integration of content areas might be accomplished through the use of the language-experience approach.

Organizing for Content-Area Integration

The first step in integrating the language arts with other subjects is to use the topics of other curriculum areas as the basis for dictated stories. When this strategy is used, children discuss and dictate about key concepts in science, social studies, mathematics, health, etc.; the dictated accounts reinforce content-area learning while also serving as the basic materials for developing reading skills. This procedure allows for increased flexibility of scheduling throughout the day to accomplish a wide variety of language arts–social studies (or language arts–science, etc.) activities. There is no longer a need to schedule "reading," "social studies," and "science" separately—the instructional activities will allow for the development of language arts skills while the main goals of the subject matter curriculum are also being met.

As an example, consider the topic of "Community Helpers," a common unit of study in first-grade social studies. A number of different community-service roles are usually introduced to the class: police officer, firefighter, mail carrier, trash collector, etc. We will use one role (police officer) to illustrate the way time could be scheduled and the kinds of activities that might be included in the first days of an integrated unit (see the chart on page 108). We will assume that the teacher has three groups of children, each one of which regularly dictates stories following the usual language-experience procedures.

SAMPLE PLAN

Community Helpers: Police Officer
Objective: To introduce children to the functions and
activities of a local police officer

MONDAY	Group A	Group B	Group C
9:00–9:30 A.M.	Local police officer visits class to describe work and discuss with children role in the community		
9:30–10:00 A.M.	Dictate account on police officer's visit	Independent activities*	
10:00–10:30 A.M.	Independent activities*	Dictate	Independent activities*
1:00–1:30 P.M.	Independent activities*		Dictate
1:30–2:00 P.M.	Review discussion with class on what was learned from day's activities; have two or three children from each dictating group read aloud that group's story to the whole class (with teacher help); have individuals share pictures, creative writing, skits, and other products resulting from the day's independent work sessions		
TUESDAY 9:00–9:30 A.M.	Reread chart story with teacher help	Independent activities*	
9:30–10:00 A.M.	Independent activities*	Reread chart story with teacher help	Independent activities*
10:30–11:00 A.M	Class views film on police officers' work		
1:00–1:30 P.M.	Independent activities*		Reread chart story with teacher help
1:30–2:00 P.M.	Teacher-directed reading-skill lesson	Independent activities*	

*See the list of independent activities below.

The following independent activities would be included in the children's programs at different times throughout the various days, depending on daily needs and interests:

Underline known words in dictated story.
Work on various word-bank activities.
Work on various word-attack activities.

Browse/read books dealing with police work.

View filmstrips on police work.

Listen to taped account of a police officer describing police work.

Plan a skit to dramatize a police officer on the job.

Make puppets to represent police officers; plan a puppet show.

Write a story about a police officer's job.

Write a thank-you note to the local police officer who visited the class.

Read other groups' dictated accounts of the police officer's visit.

Read own dictated account of officer's visit to others.

Draw a series of pictures to illustrate police officers at work.

We have charted only two days here, since the purpose of the illustration is to suggest some scheduling procedures and activities that integrate the two curriculum areas. Somewhat more time would be needed, of course, to reinforce the sight vocabulary and other reading skills related to the dictated story. The usual amount of time would be spent on meeting these reading instructional goals. More time could also be spent on other activities related to the social studies goal of acquainting children with the role of the police officer in the community. (More or less time could be devoted to all these activities depending on the number of other content-area lessons and activities to be accomplished.)

Scheduling of time is flexible; on some days more time can be spent developing specific reading skills while on other days more time can be spent meeting the objectives of the social studies curriculum. But there is purposely no "reading time" or "social studies time" in the schedule; most of the time children will be working on a variety of activities that develop skills and knowledge in both areas.

A second example provides an idea of the kinds of reading materials that might grow out of such an integrated unit of study. In this instance, a first-grade teacher recognized that the class was especially interested in animals. She decided to devote a number of weeks to the study of different animals so that children could learn about their habitats, eating patterns and so on. A typical lesson plan included the following steps:

1. On Friday afternoon the teacher presented a variety of pictures of the "animal of the week" to the class as a whole. Pictures from *National Geographic*, *Ranger Rick*, and other nature magazines were used as well as some films or filmstrips.

2. On Monday the teacher led discussions in each reading group about the chosen animal, giving children information about the animal and sometimes reading aloud particularly interesting parts of magazine articles. The children asked questions and made comments during this time.

3. The teacher took dictated stories from the different reading groups. These stories included information the children had learned through the class discussion. The children were not expected to include all the information that had been discussed. The teacher only suggested they think of some things they had learned about the animal.

4. Time was spent during the week following the usual procedures of the language-experience approach to build reading skills.

5. All week the children had the opportunity to read each other's group stories, look at the pictures displayed in the room, and view films and filmstrips about the animal. The same kinds of independent activities were used in these units as were suggested for the community helpers unit described earlier.

Following are three group-dictated stories that were obtained during units organized in this way. The teacher decided not to include the children's names with their contributions in order to make the accounts seem more like expository, informative material. The children had made good progress with the language-experience approach and thus did not need the extra help of having their names included with their contributions.

THE BATS

They fly at night with their babies sometimes. The vampire bat eats a tablespoon of blood. They see with their ears. They fly with their hands. The fruit bats eat fruit. Bats are pretty. Fox bats hang on trees. They live in caves. They take them into the labs to study about them. We like bats.

KING CRAB

The ice is frozen on the ships that catch king crabs. They catch king crabs because men, women and children like to eat them. They like to eat their food

alive. They live in water and hatch out of
eggs. It is cold in the water. They can live
25 years. They have ten legs. They weigh
ten pounds.

OLIVE SEA SNAKES

Olive sea snakes are dangerous. If the
snake bites you, you are dead cause
there is no antivenom. The lungs are long.
They can kill you. The olive sea snake kills
fish. They are poisonous. They stay under
water for a long time.

Much more information was presented, discussed, and learned
about each animal than these stories include. The dictated stories
were used primarily to develop reading skills; reinforcement of
learning about the animal was an important, though secondary, goal
while the groups were working on reading skills. However, the
stories do reflect acquisition of much interesting information, and
the other activities related to the topics (e.g., filmstrips) provided
for learning of basic information and concepts.

As the week progressed, there were good opportunities to
make comparisons among the various animals studied and so to
extend learning considerably. Some of the children in the class
became interested in the concept of endangered species and
learned the hows and whys of deciding that a given animal should
be considered in danger of extinction. With the teacher's help several children wrote to government agencies and authors of
magazine articles to ask for further information about various endangered species and to express their opinions and concerns about
favorite animals.

These are only two examples of the integration of content-area
studies with the language-experience program. There are many
other possibilities. This integrated approach emphasizes the importance of reading in all curricular areas and provides interesting and
worthwhile topics for dictation.

THE USE OF LANGUAGE-EXPERIENCE IN KINDERGARTEN

The flexibility inherent in the language-experience approach
makes it ideal for developing prereading skills in kindergarten. It is

generally agreed that one of the most important prereading skills is competence with oral language. Children need opportunities to use language actively as they describe firsthand experiences. They need to play with language, developing an ear for the sounds of rhyme and alliteration. Children also need to learn that there is a connection between spoken and written language, that their words can be written down to be read again and again. Kindergarten teachers will find that these needs can be met within a language-experience program.

In kindergarten the focal point of a language-experience activity should be the examination of the stimulus or interesting experience. Children's vocabulary can be expanded as they discuss something that is tasted, smelled, squeezed, or compared with other objects. Children can also learn new concepts while they are acquiring the language to talk about their world. With the emphasis on discussion, the dictation and subsequent rereading become a summary activity. Children see their words, vivid with recent associations, written on the chart to be read and reread. In this way language development and an awareness of the function of reading can both be accomplished.

Although the use of language-experience can be justified for kindergarten children as a form of good readiness instruction, it can also be justified when it provides continuity of instruction in schools where children will be participating in language-experience programs in first grade. In the early stages of language arts/reading instruction, consistency is important. Once children grow accustomed to a mode of instruction, it is advantageous to provide for continuity.

Procedures

Earlier chapters have dealt with methods for stimulating oral language, for recording dictated stories, and for providing follow-up activities. Kindergarten teachers can use many of the techniques suggested. However, some adjustments in the general procedures may help tailor language-experience to meet the differing needs of kindergarten children.

Grouping. Usually kindergarten children are randomly grouped for oral language activities and for story dictation. This permits children who lack a ready facility with language to hear and to imitate more verbal youngsters. Heterogeneous grouping also increases the likelihood that some children in the group will wish to contribute to a dictated story.

Individualization of instruction really occurs after the story chart is completed. Activities can include rereading as well as visual and auditory discrimination of letters, sounds, and words; children learn what is personally meaningful to them and what they are most ready to learn. Some individuals in the group may be at an early stage in which they are learning to recognize what the process of reading is. Other individuals may be ready to learn the difference between upper- and lower-case letters; others may recognize and remember individual words. Of course, some children may learn to read as well as the typical first-grade child. All children are being simultaneously exposed to the same experience, but each child is learning what he is ready to learn.

Language-experience activities with kindergartners are usually more successful if groups are limited to five or six children. Small groups make it easier to engage all the children in a discussion and also to complete the dictation and rereading before their attention begins to wander. It is quite possible, given the varied degrees of maturity among kindergarten children, that all children will not choose to dictate or even be attentive during the dictating activity. Children should nevertheless be allowed to be passive participants, for the day will come for each of them to say, "It's time for my name now." We suggest, therefore, that all be encouraged to participate in the examination of the stimulus, dictating, and rereading. If, however, there are youngsters whose attention span has been expended by the time for recording dictation, perhaps it is wise to let them slip away to do something else. It is better to maintain a casual atmosphere in which interest is the prime motivator than to require participation. If children have positive feelings about the language-experience activity, they will eventually want to be part of it.

Recording Dictation. The form of recording kindergarten children's dictation does not differ from the form used with first-grade children. Children's names introduce their sentences, as: Joey said, "We saw the kitty purr." It is so rewarding for children to see their own names printed on the chart that often this is the primary motivation for dictating. Furthermore, if names are consistently used to start recorded contributions, names will come to serve as a cue for the beginning of sentences.

When recording children's dictation, it is important to record their exact language using standard punctuation. Children need to see that their language can be written down for someone else to read. If the teacher edits their sentences, they will not see the match between what they said and what is read.

In one classroom we have seen the teacher sometimes act as a scribe, recording children's spontaneous language while they play. By the time the youngsters have begun to tire of playing, several of their sentences have been recorded on a chart. Children who have been drifting in and out of the play activity are gathered together. The teacher then says, "Look, we can read what you've said." By eliminating the step where all the children are expected to quietly watch the recording, this teacher extends the time for reading the chart. This variation is not recommended as a regular alternative, but it does illustrate how a teacher can be flexible with language-experience procedures and so cope with the brief attention span of some kindergartners.

Another alternative to the standard procedure is for a large-group activity to serve as a language stimulus. For instance, a classroom visitor, a walk in the woods, or a visit to another area of the school, in which all children participate at once, can all be used as stimuli. At a later time dictation can be taken from small groups. By dividing the oral language/concept-development activity and the dictating/reading activity, it is sometimes easier to maintain young children's interest.

Scheduling

There is no one way to schedule LEA in a kindergarten classroom. Some teachers always use a dictated story to summarize any oral language activity. Their classrooms are literally plastered with story charts—directions for caring for the gerbils, stories about trips around the school, recipes for classroom cooking. Other teachers like to plan for dictated stories on a regular schedule, perhaps once or twice a week. Some teachers plan for rereading a story and follow-up activities as part of the daily schedule. Others prefer to use playtime, informally gathering those children who are most able to reread dictated stories.

One teacher we know systematically plans for concept development using language-experience as a summary activity. She schedules two related activities per week. This gives children an opportunity to examine and expand their understanding of such varied topics as fish, snow, or fire engines. In the illustration following, this teacher used a drum as a stimulus; this example shows how this practice provided for language development, allowed children to explore a concept, and yielded a tangible accomplishment, a dictated story book.

On Monday, the children played with the drum, taking turns

beating it and marching to the beat, using the words *drumsticks*, *beat*, *rhythm*, and *march*. After playing and marching, the following story was dictated:

DRUMS

Joe said, "I beat the drum." Sissy said, "I like to play the drum." Michele said, "The drum is round." Margie said, "I beat the drum with sticks." Dick said, "Drums are noisy."

On Tuesday, the children gathered to reread the story with the teacher. She first read it aloud, and then the children read it with her, following her voice. This was repeated several times. On this particular occasion, the teacher decided to give some practice identifying upper- and lower-case letters. She asked questions like:

Who can find a capital *D*?
Who can find a small *d*?
Who can find a small *n*?
Who can find a small *b*?
Who can find another small *b*?
What's the capital letter in the first line?
How many capital *M*s are there?

On Wednesday the teacher played a record of marching music. After listening to the record, the children listened for the drumbeat, clapped the beat, and finally marched around the room in step with the beat of the music. Again when the children gathered in small groups there was an opportunity to discuss the activity using words like *drum*, *beat*, *rhythm*, and *march*. The children dictated the following story:

DRUM MUSIC

Sissy said, "I marched to the music." Dick said, "I could hear the drum." Chris said, "I like the drum." Joe said, "The music feels good." Margie said, "The music feels noisy." Michele said, "I like the music."

On Thursday, the small group of children gathered to read their new story with the teacher. The same procedure was followed as before. The teacher read the story to the group and then they "read" it with her several times. The teacher then hung the first story, "Drums," beside the new story, "Drum Music." She reread it to the children and then had them read with her. Again the children searched for upper- and lower-case letters, but this time they used both story charts. At the close of the activity, they chorally read both drum stories.

Although she did not always make a practice of giving each child a copy of the group-dictated story, on Friday of this week the teacher gave each one a page containing both stories. The children drew pictures to illustrate their "drum book." These pictures were stapled to make a cover for the two stories, which were then ready to be taken home.

The original drum stories were placed on a chart rack with the drum stories dictated by other groups of children. This chart rack was so constructed that the stories hung at the children's eye level, and the charts were positioned so that the children could easily move them. From time to time there were requests for the teacher or other adults in the room to reread these stories.

Follow-up Activities

Language-experience needs to be handled with a light touch in kindergarten. Children's attention spans may be short and their facility with language varied. Consequently, rather than always using the story charts for structured prereading skill development, teachers can view the story charts as one of many resources when teaching. For instance, the concept of upper- and lower-case letters can be taught using the chart, or key words chosen from a story chart can be used when practicing auditory and auditory-visual discrimination (see pages 45–46). But working with one chart story until all the instructional possibilities have been exhausted is not the goal; rather, children should be talking about many topics and dictating many story charts.

Because children like to return to favorite stories, we urge teachers to make chart stories readily available. Stories can be taped on the walls at the children's eye level, placed on a chart rack for easy perusal, or bound in giant books to spread on the floor for reading. Some teachers bind copies of stories, perhaps five or six stories to a book, for placement on the library table. One teacher we know makes enough books for the classroom library so that at the end of the year each child can have a book to keep.

Other follow-up activities can include showing filmstrips, reading stories aloud, and obtaining books for the library table—all on the same general topic as the current dictated stories. Surrounding children with language, spoken and written, giving children a sense of accomplishment in language activities, stimulating children's interest in books and reading—these are all functions of a language-experience kindergarten.

LANGUAGE-EXPERIENCE AS A SUPPLEMENT TO A BASAL PROGRAM

Language-experience can be a support program for those children beyond first grade who need slow-paced reading instruction. These are children who need more opportunities for reinforcement of sight vocabulary and word-attack skills than is usually provided in a basal reading program. This slower pace, while necessary for mastery, may cause children's enthusiasm for any given basal story to wane. One way to maintain children's interest in reading is to supplement the basal reader with language-experience activities.

Interesting, often concrete, story stimuli that can be manipulated as well as discussed can yield dictated stories rich in associations that can aid retention of sight vocabulary. In addition, stories usually contain many high-frequency words which in isolation have low meaning value. These often troublesome words occur repeatedly in meaningful contexts, thus giving children opportunities for overlearning. Also, children's reading of their own dictation often builds self-confidence and increases reading fluency.

To implement a meld of basal reader and language-experience, a teacher might reserve certain days for each teacher-directed activity and schedule independent language-experience follow-up in learning centers. A schedule could be as follows:

Day 1   Lesson with story in basal reader
Day 2   Teacher-directed follow-up basal reader story
Day 3   Dictated story
Day 4   Rereading story; word-attack lesson using dictated story chart
Day 5   Sight word games and other skill activities

Independent activities could include:

Workbook skill pages
Learning centers with word card activities (see chapter 4 for suggestions)
Independent reading of classroom library materials
Creative writing

When using language-experience to supplement instruction, teachers can experiment with different aspects. We once saw some exciting reading instruction in a third-grade classroom where the teacher planned simple science experiments for oral language stimuli. She recorded group dictation, gave children copies of the story, and used the story chart for a variety of teacher-directed activities. However, instead of having children underline known words and collect word cards, she gave each child a sheet of paper divided into blocks, each block containing one word from the story. The children cut these word blocks apart and filed them in an envelope labeled with the name of the story. The word cards were then available to use for independent activities and sight word games.

The following stories are samples of dictation from this group of third graders, who were reading significantly below the third-grade level. The topics illustrate the kinds of concrete experiences used to provoke interest and discussion among these youngsters. These children, like many others for whom learning to read is a slow process, responded better to objects they could handle than to more abstract experiences.

THE TASTE TEST

There were three cups that had A, B, and C. Harry and Bart said, "C had a cup taste and didn't really taste very good." Janeen said, "C and A tasted pretty good against B which tasted sour." Most of the kids liked Wyler's best. Cheeri-aid is not popular but our kids like it better than Kool-Aid.

February 3

THE LITTLE TRAIN

The trains go fast and slow. The train has power. The cars are different from each other. The caboose is the last one in the whole train. The trains are very small. The track is very small. The train goes under the tunnel. The transformer controls the train.

February 25

THE MOUSETRAP

It was hard to set it. It is dangerous. It hurts
when the mouse gets caught. The mouse
likes cheese. The mouse goes after the
cheese and he gets caught. It's faster to
get put out of your misery in a mousetrap
than it is by a cat. You'd better watch out
for the mousetrap when it's set.

March 19

LANGUAGE-EXPERIENCE FOR REMEDIAL INSTRUCTION

Language-experience can be used with the child who is severely retarded in reading, who has experienced conventional instruction but has not learned to read. Reacting to repeated failure,
the disabled reader generally dislikes and avoids reading tasks and
books. The language-experience approach, however, can give this
reader success in activities with written words because LEA
capitalizes on the child's interests, language, and knowledge of the
world and because it involves procedures and activities that are not
like those in the materials the child used previously.

Language-experience for the disabled reader is one-to-one individualized instruction and is usually used by a private tutor or in
a clinical program. The average classroom teacher frequently finds
it difficult to schedule this intensive one-to-one instruction on a
regular basis. However, for the teacher who can schedule tutorial
sessions or direct an aide or volunteer working with a disabled
reader, we will outline language-experience procedures modified
for remedial instruction.

The first step is to identify the child's interests, which will
determine the topics for dictation. The teacher may find a filmstrip
on moon probes to use as a stimulus for a space-crazy youngster or
may introduce directions for making paper-clip jewelry with
another. For some children story after story will be dictated on the
same favorite topic; this may mean limited interests or a genuine
reluctance to dictate on any subject other than a "safe" one. Since
the goal is to develop reading skills, the content of the stories is
relatively unimportant. If the topic is of interest to the child, there
will usually be a willingness to discuss and to dictate, and, furthermore, many words will be remembered because of their pleasant

associations. The following stories illustrate this adherence to one topic.

AFTER SUPPER

After supper I tie a string around a ball,
and then I throw it and Pepper runs after it.
He likes to chew it. And then I pull it and
Pepper doesn't know where it went. And
then he runs all around trying to find the
ball.   *April 2*

MY DOG PEPPER

When I come home from school, I play
with my dog. I pull his tail around by his
stomach. Then he goes around in circles
real, real fast. And he tries to bite my
hand, and then when I'm done he bites
my feet. And then he gets tired and sticks
his tongue out and lays on the floor and
swishes his tail and cleans the kitchen
floor.   *April 5*

HERE WE GO AGAIN ON PEPPER

Last night it was hot and Pepper was hot.
So he went in the bathroom and jumped
into the bathtub. And then in the morning,
Mom got up and she saw Pepper in the
bathtub. And he didn't put his head up or
open his eyes. He just lay still as a rug. Then
in about fifteen minutes Pepper got out of
the bathtub. And then she said, "I'll clean
the bathtub out tonight."   *April 16*

Dictation is recorded using the child's language but omitting the child's name. After transcribing, the teacher reads the account aloud, saying, "Tell me if this says what you want it to say." In this manner the child is given an opportunity to edit according to the sound of his language; a youngster will frequently make corrections at this point. Following this rereading of the story, the procedure for remedial LEA varies from the developmental approach previously outlined. Because the intitial emphasis is on teaching sight words, the approach for learning words is very structured.

In lieu of having the child underline known words, three lists are prepared for each story: a sequential list and two scrambled lists.*

1. A sequential list is the story typed in list form with all capitalization retained.
2. Scramble I is a list of all the words known at sight on the sequential list. Duplicate words are omitted and the word order is changed.
3. Scramble II is a list of all the words known at sight on the Scramble I list with the word order again changed. Words known on the Scramble II list are written on word cards.

See Appendix B for illustrations of each of the above.

With each list the words are briefly exposed one at a time for the child to pronounce. This flashing of words can be accomplished by covering the preceding and following words in the list with a file card held in each hand. The cards can be slid together to cover a word and slightly parted to expose it very briefly. Each word the child reads at sight is noted. The teacher can give help identifying unknown words by referring to the story context or suggesting other word-attack skills.

A five-day sequence would be as follows:

Day 1   Discussion and dictation
Day 2   Rereading of story; flashed presentation of sequential list
Day 3   Rereading of story; flashed presentation of Scramble I
Day 4   Flashed presentation of Scramble II
Day 5   Word cards

Table 11 is a weekly schedule incorporating the activities in this five-day sequence. It is one example of how a child's program can be planned each week.

This framework for remedial LEA needs to be supplemented with additional language arts activities appropriate to the child's achievement level. These might include:

*This particular use of structured lists as story follow-up is a clinical procedure that we learned from Russell G. Stauffer. It was part of the procedure of clinical LEA instruction at The Reading-Study Center, University of Delaware, while Dr. Stauffer was director of the center.

Table 11
Schedule for Three-Week Remedial LEA

Week	Monday	Tuesday	Wednesday	Thursday	Friday
1	Dictate story[1]*	Reread story[1]	Reread story[1]	Scramble II[1]	Word cards[1]
		Sequential list[1]	Scramble I[1]	Dictate story[2]	Sequential list[2]
2	Reread story[2]	Scramble II[2]	Word cards[2]	Reread story[3]	Scramble II[3]
	Scramble I[2]	Dictate story[3]	Reread story[3]	Scramble I[3]	**
			Sequential list[3]		
3	Word cards[3]	Reread story[4]	Reread story[4]	Scramble II[4]	Word cards[4]
	Dictate story[5]	Sequential list[4]	Scramble I[4]	Dictate story[5]	Reread story[5]
					Sequential list[5]

*For easy reference, each dictated story and all materials generated from that story are identified by the story number. Stories are numbered chronologically.

**No new story dictation.

Word-card activities and games
Teacher-made games to reinforce sight words
Creative writing
Teacher reading
Independent reading in trade books
Newspaper reading
Choral reading with teacher

Initially in a remedial program, the language-experience approach can provide the major part of reading instruction. Gradually, however, as the child begins to read in books, LEA will become the supplementary activity. Its value beyond the beginning reading stage is that it maintains the link between the child's interests and learning to read. It provides an easy means for the child to learn and read at sight words of high interest or need.*

SUMMARY

The basic principles of the language-experience approach can be applied in several areas of elementary curriculum and instruction. Individually dictated stories can be used in many situations to help children with special needs or to provide variety in a basic first-grade LEA program. With LEA as a framework, language arts instruction can be integrated with other content areas at several grade levels, providing an overall curriculum that demonstrates the importance of language arts in all areas. LEA can be adapted to kindergarten classes and provide some particularly valuable approaches to oral language development and other readiness skills. As a supplement to a basal program or as a basis of a remedial program, the language-experience approach has many advantages. While especially useful as a beginning program, LEA can be extended to these other areas to maintain and improve sound reading instruction.

*A more detailed explanation of language-experience used as a remedial technique can be found in R. G. Stauffer, J. Abrams, and J. J. Pikulski, *Diagnosis, Correction and Prevention of Reading Disabilities* (New York: Harper & Row, 1978).

Chapter VII

The Continuing Program

Dictated stories, word-bank activities, and other procedures already described are only the beginning steps of the language-experience approach to reading. As children progress through these first stages, the teacher must plan the continuing program, anticipating the need to increase the variety and quantity of reading materials available to the children and the need to provide for the individual differences that will arise. The teacher should attend to the following aspects of the continuing language-experience program:

1. Encouraging use of the classroom library
2. Helping children make the transition to basal readers
3. Using informal assessments of progress
4. Providing for individual differences

ENCOURAGING USE OF THE CLASSROOM LIBRARY

Most children come to school expecting to learn to read and will soon learn to read their own dictated stories in a language-experience program. Their motivation to read will be aroused from the first in this way. This motivation can be maintained by providing pleasant, successful experiences with books. For some youngsters the classroom library may represent their first experience with a collection of reading material. Their first opportunity to examine various reading materials and to read books on many topics can mark the beginning of habits of wide reading.

It is important from the very beginning of reading instruction to develop habits of wide reading. Exposure to a variety of topics gives children the opportunity to broaden their background of information in many areas. It also provides for meaningful practice of word-attack skills and for the reinforcement of sight vocabulary. As children practice wide reading, they will simultaneously improve in reading skill and in knowledge of their world. The classroom library can provide the impetus for this reading in many materials.

From the first week of school to the end of the year, the classroom library should be a center of attention in a language-experience classroom. We recommend a spacious and, if possible, central location. A low table on which to display materials attractively is useful. More books can be displayed on other tables or shelves nearby. Comfortable chairs or floor cushions can be provided to make the area attractive and inviting.

Figure 33:   Classroom library

Children need ample time every day to use the classroom library for a variety of purposes: to browse, to look at picture books, to find known words in any material, to read for amusement and information. Many children will be eager to pursue books and, if given adequate opportunities, will not need further encouragement to read. Some children, however, will need some prodding to select books and read for pleasure. All children will undoubtedly profit from a teacher who shows enthusiasm for reading and makes a special effort to encourage children to read often.

Materials

Attention should be given to selecting appropriate materials for the library area. One important consideration is to provide an ample variety of different types of materials to suit the tastes and interests of the different children in the class. All materials will not be read with the same depth of understanding or for the same purposes. Some books will be enjoyed for their eye-catching illustrations alone, and children may simply like looking at the pictures or discussing the illustrations with other children. Some books will be used for browsing for known words, and though children may not follow the story line or understand the topic, they may recognize some familiar words. Other materials will be read carefully and thoroughly, with good understanding of the topic or story line. Some books will be used for a few moments and then exchanged for others; some will be read or looked at for a long time.

Teachers need to devote special care to introducing children to the pleasure of dipping into many different kinds of materials, reading for many different purposes. We recommend including the following kinds of materials in the library area:

Fiction books
Nonfiction books
Picture books
Magazines
Newspapers
Collections of dictated stories from different groups
Preprimers from a variety of different basal series
Book/record sets (or cassettes) for reading-listening
Comic books
Poetry books

Such an assortment of materials should also suit the levels of reading achievement found among children in a typical classroom.

Some children will have come to school with well-developed reading skills or will have made rapid progress in the language-experience program. These more advanced readers, if given the chance, may profitably pursue many books which might at first be thought too difficult for them. Other children who may be making slow progress in learning to read will enjoy and profit most from picture books and other materials with good illustrations. Thus, it is important in a classroom library to provide not only variety of content but a range of difficulty. For instance, books written at pre-primer through second- or third-grade level can be displayed; art reproduction or photography books are often popular; an animal encyclopedia or other such reference materials might be included; a wide selection of children's and adults' magazines can also provide good browsing and reading materials.

Many, if not most, of the materials should be easy-to-read selections which will not frustrate beginning readers who have minimal word-recognition skills. These easy-to-read books in which children practice their learned reading skills can provide a transition from dictated stories to stories in a basal reader. Many titles are available for the beginning reader. Titles of some easy books are given in Appendix C. A list of easy-to-read series is given in Appendix D. These are not exhaustive lists but include titles we have read and judged appropriate for children who are just beginning to read books. Appendix E gives a suggested list of picture books for children who have not yet learned to recognize words and for others who might enjoy them as well.

Procedures

To motivate children to use the classroom library and to encourage a general interest in reading, we have found the following teacher practices useful:

1. *Add new materials to the library area frequently.* A number of new selections should be made available every week. Children are more likely to be attracted to the library area and find something to interest them if fresh materials are always available. Some titles, of course, may be returned to the area after a period of absence; a new interest may be aroused at any time for a particular book, or children may have "old favorites" that they wish to read several times throughout the year.
2. *Display materials attractively.* Books that are shelved or piled in a heap are not as inviting as books that are displayed well.

Some books can be placed on the table so the titles are easily seen; others can be lined up on a nearby shelf; still others might be hung from the ceiling at eye level, using heavy string and large clips.

Sometimes special groupings can be made relating to a current topic of interest. For instance, a collection of materials on dinosaurs or rocks or monsters can be displayed together. For such special displays other objects or pictures might be included. A collection of books on shells, for instance, will be even more attractive if a few real shells are placed in the display.

3. *Give regular book talks.* Take a few minutes several times a week to call attention to materials in the library area. Describe the contents of various books; show illustrations in magazines that the children might enjoy examining; suggest reading materials that might strike the interest of particular children.

4. *Read aloud to children daily.* Choose books on a wide variety of topics that will appeal to the interests and tastes of the children. Some materials should be short enough to be read at one sitting; others may be chosen for reading over a period of days. The teacher's enthusiasm for the story or book can spark the children's interest, and the pleasure of listening to a good tale or interesting account can further motivate interest in books and reading.

5. *Tape some favorite read-aloud books.* Children rapidly acquire favorite read-aloud stories and ask to hear them over and over. Capitalize on this interest by making cassette tapes of some of the available stories. Place a book and its accompanying tape in a drawstring bag to keep them together. If a tape recorder and earphones are available, children can listen to the stories while looking at the illustrations and following the book's text.

6. *Plan regular "free-reading" times for all children.* One of the best but frequently neglected independent activities in the reading program is browsing/reading. Some teachers plan a single free-reading session every day, at which time all the children in the room are expected to look at or read books and other materials. Such a whole-class reading period is one very good way of encouraging children to become involved with books. However, children can also be assigned additional free-reading time as a regular part of their programs, just as they are assigned time to work at learning stations or to complete skill-training activities.

7. *Make sharing a regular part of the reading program.* Giving children the chance to talk about the things they have read can stimulate others' interests in reading. Children will often be

encouraged to look at or read books that their peers have read and enjoyed. Also, regular sharing periods will demonstrate that reading is valued as a worthwhile activity. Children do not need to write book reports or give formal book talks, but they can be encouraged periodically and frequently to tell their classmates what they are reading and enjoying.

8. *Encourage children to read to each other.* Interest in reading can often be stimulated by encouraging children to read aloud to one another for short periods of time. Children should be allowed to choose the materials they wish to read and can also be encouraged to choose their own partners for such sharing. Some children may establish special "buddies," and such regular partners can always profit from listening to and reading to one another. At other times the teacher may suggest new pairings for various reasons. Such a procedure, for instance, can enable the children with less well-developed skills to enjoy stories that their more advanced peers are able to read.

Although the classroom library is an important part of a language-experience classroom from the first day of school, its importance becomes more evident as the year progresses and children increase their reading abilities through the use of their dictated stories. Sight vocabularies and other reading skills can be developed more effectively through the use of a wide variety of materials once basic skills have been learned. Thus, the continuing program must allow for continued exposure to a wide variety of reading materials.

HELPING CHILDREN MAKE THE TRANSITION TO BASAL READERS

As we discussed in the Introduction, one of the goals of a language-experience program is to provide a solid foundation of sight vocabulary and word-attack and comprehension skills that will allow children to profit from formal reading instruction using materials other than dictated stories. Such formal instruction can often best be accomplished with the primer and first reader of a basal series.* Some children will be ready for this instruction early

*Because basal series differ somewhat in terms of distinguishing between a *primer* and a *first reader*, we use both terms here. We find that most teachers use LEA procedures until children seem ready for the first hardback book in the basal series, which may be a primer or a first reader depending on the series.

in the school year, after a few weeks or a few months of following the language-experience procedures outlined in earlier chapters. Other children will require more time to develop the prerequisite skills and will be ready for a first reader by January or February of the school year. Other children may still be developing the necessary skills at the end of the school year. In the continuing language-experience program the teacher must know when and how to help children make the transition from dictated stories and related activities to the basal series used in the classroom.

In a basal approach to beginning reading children are moved through various levels of materials (the readiness book, the pre-primers, etc.). Progress is measured by assessing the rate with which children complete these graded materials, and children can be classified according to the level of materials they are using, e.g., "the preprimer group." Children are usually moved into a first reader when they have completed teacher-directed lessons in the preprimers and primer of the basal series. In a language-experience program, however, since dictated stories are the reading materials, children are not considered to be at "first preprimer level" or "second preprimer level" as they are in the initial stages of a basal reader program. The language-experience approach, an individualized, essentially nongraded program, requires other ways of recognizing progress and incorporating a basal reader into the overall program.

Rather than categorizing children according to a basal level, teachers in a language-experience program observe the specific skills that children have or acquire and gradually modify lessons and activities to enable children to move with ease from dictated stories to commercially prepared preprimers to the first hardback book in the series. Some guidelines are needed to make the proper judgments, however. First, teachers must recognize the skills, behaviors, and attitudes that mark the point at which children are ready to begin the transition into basal materials for formal basal instruction. When a child meets the following criteria, he or she has reached the beginning of this transition stage:

1. The child is able to read past and current dictated stories independently with a high degree of accuracy.
2. The child can identify some unfamiliar words with the aid of word-attack skills (context clues, phonics, etc.).
3. The child has approximately 150 different word-bank words.

4. The child is able to encode ideas in creative writing attempts with a good degree of phonological accuracy.
5. The child shows an interest in library table materials and has read several easy-to-read books independently.

These skills, behaviors, and attitudes indicate that the child has made good progress in the initial stages of the language-experience approach and has acquired a good foundation for work in other reading materials. At this point, however, it is not wise to move the child immediately into a basal reader and eliminate dictated stories and their related skill activities from the reading program. To do so can often result in frustration for the child, since the basal reader and accompanying activities are usually in sharp contrast to the initial language-experience activities that have allowed the child so much chance for success.

At this time, dictation, rereading, and the regular skill development activities should be continued, but time spent on these basic procedures should be reduced somewhat to allow for transition-stage activities. Most importantly, work needs to be done to widen exposure to a variety of materials read for different purposes and to increase the application of word-attack skills.

Widening Exposure to Published Materials

Children at the transition stage will have begun to read some easy materials independently, but this reading will largely have been to reinforce sight vocabulary and to build interest in books and other materials. Children will have spent more time browsing through books and using books to find known words than reading whole books from beginning to end. Most of their reading will have included their own and peers' dictated accounts, which deal with familiar topics and are written in familiar language patterns. At this point children need to read more widely and purposefully in preparation for dealing with the group-reading activities that are the core of a basal program. Wide reading of published materials will allow children to make the transition from reading their own language patterns to reading materials written by an unfamiliar, relatively remote author. Their purposes for reading can also be widened to include following a story line, seeking information, grasping details and main ideas, anticipating events in a narrative account, and other skills of comprehension that will be needed in dealing with the basal materials.

To introduce children to a greater number of purposes for reading and to provide experiences with different types of published materials, the activities suggested below should be used. At least a half hour a day should be devoted to one or more of these activities:

1. Have different children in the group read different books for the purpose of retelling the story to the group. The child who is retelling the story can use the book itself as a "prop" to show some of the illustrations to the rest of the group as the story is retold.
2. If two or three children have read the same book, have them plan to act out the story for the rest of the group.
3. When a child finishes reading a book, have him or her draw an illustration of a favorite scene. The child can describe the scene to the teacher verbally when the illustration is completed, and the teacher can write the description in a sentence or two at the bottom of the illustration. A number of these illustrations can be displayed in the room.
4. When a child has finished reading a self-chosen book, have that child read a portion of the book aloud to the rest of the group. A favorite scene can be chosen to share in this way.
5. Introduce a number of different nonfiction books to the group. Have each child choose the book he or she would like to read. Have each child in the group state one fact that he or she would like to find out about the topic. Have the children read their books to see if they can find the information they are interested in. When everyone has finished, gather the group together to review the prereading questions and have each child tell what he or she learned from reading the book.

Since a major goal at this time is to provide materials that children will be able to read comfortably, the teacher must be sure to make available a number of easy-to-read materials. There should be enough different titles available to provide each child a choice of two or three books a week. Preprimers from several basal series can be made available, including the preprimers from the series that will be used later for formal instruction. It is neither necessary nor desirable, however, to provide a copy of each book for each child in this transition stage; if there are ten children at this stage, ten copies of the same title are not needed. We emphasize this point because we have found that teachers just learning to use language-experience procedures often feel compelled to have all the children in a transition group read the same preprimer at the same time under teacher supervision. These teachers express concern that the children need to be "put in a book" so that their reading achievement level can be described in terms of the level of the book and also so that the children will be "prepared" for work in that basal series' primer or first reader.

We reject the argument that children need to be "put in a book" at this stage for a number of reasons. First, almost every preprimer on the market today has such a carefully controlled and limited vocabulary that the stories are weak in plot, dialogue, and character development. The language is stilted and, more importantly, often unnecessary to read because the abundant pictures tell the whole story, or most of it, anyway, In comparison with the rich language and interesting topics of children's own dictated stories, preprimer stories are pale and insignificant. Also, since the stories are short and usually very simple, there is very little to discuss or speculate about in a group setting. The typical preprimer lesson is highly teacher directed, involving many literal recall questions, e.g., Who saw the turtle first? What did Sandy find in her room? Children read a few words and answer several recall questions; there is little opportunity for the exercise of higher-level thinking skills. The main goals in such lessons are to make sure the children recognize the words correctly and pay reasonable attention to the story line. Such lessons do not allow reading to be exciting or informative; hence, motivation is predictably low in most groups exposed to this type of instruction. During this transition stage preprimers can be made available for independent reading, but they should not be used for group lessons as described in the preprimer teacher's manual.

When made available for independent reading, preprimers can be used by transition-stage readers to practice learned reading skills and to reinforce and extend sight vocabulary. Children can read stories in these books to each other or can read whole books on their own. Most transition-stage readers will be able to read a preprimer at one or two sittings, less time, actually, than they would spend if they were moving through the book under manual-directed teacher supervision. Children can ask each other and the teacher for help with any unknown words or they can use their developing word-attack skills to analyze words on their own. While these materials are not substantive enough for teacher-directed group reading lessons, they are quite satisfactory for children who need exposure to a variety of easy materials that they are allowed to handle at their own rates. The greater the variety of books at these levels (from a number of different basal series) that are provided, the greater the chance to exercise developing word-attack skills.

By involving children in the activities suggested in this section, the teacher will be able to observe pupils' abilities to handle these materials. If further checking is desired, the teacher can always have children read any portion of these books aloud. Notes can be made of any difficulties and further lessons can be planned to develop any needed skills.

Besides preprimers from basal series, other easy-to-read materials should be provided for transition-stage readers. The classroom library can be used as the main source for additional reading materials. (See Appendixes C, D, and E for suggested titles.)

To allow for more purposeful reading, the teacher may also modify the activities related to the dictated stories of the group in this transition stage. After a story has been dictated, the teacher may make up questions to accompany it. In answering the questions children will need to reread the experience story to find the particular information required by the question. Such an activity can encourage purposeful rereading of the material and give practice in locating specific information in a passage, both skills that are necessary as children work with more advanced basal materials. Below is an example of a group-dictated story and the questions that a teacher devised to accompany it.

COBRA SNAKES

They are poisonous. They live in India. The mother snake guards the eggs so nothing will kill them. They got hoods. Cobras are cousins of the olive sea snake. Baby snakes hatch out of eggs. They make things out of the skin.

1. Are they poisonous?
2. Where do they live?
3. Why does the mother snake guard the eggs?
4. They are cousins of the _____.
5. What do they make out of the skin?

Children can be asked to write in their answers or to underline the part of the story that answers the question. Or, a group can be gathered to read the questions and find the answers together.

Increasing Application of Word-Attack Skills

By the time children have reached the transition stage, they will be able to recognize many of the words that are typically used in primers and first readers. However, they may not have learned all the specific words that a particular basal series uses in its beginning reading materials (and, in fact, should not be expected to do so). Many "new" words will need to be figured out when the primer or first reader is introduced. Thus, before moving into a basal series, children will need a good amount of practice in analyzing unfamiliar words so that they will not become frustrated at encountering unknown words in the first formal book.

Of course, if regular instruction has been given in word-attack skills (see chapter 4), children will have completed many skill-training exercises and will have identified many unknown words in dictated stories. Some unfamiliar words will also have been encountered in easy-to-read library materials. These experiences will have laid a good foundation for the effective use of word-attack skills in basal materials, but additional practice in exercising these skills is needed to ensure successful dealing with the first formal book.

Activities need to be introduced at this point to enable children to gain greater proficiency in the application of word-attack skills. These activities might include such things as teacher-written materials and "word hunts."

Teacher-Written Materials

The teacher can prepare materials for transition-stage children that purposely include some words assumed to be unfamiliar to them. A short account can be prepared based on something that has recently been the topic of the children's group dictation. Many of the words from the dictated story (and from previous dictated stories) that have been learned by many of the children can be used, and a few "new" words can be introduced for practice in word analysis. Such teacher-written accounts should be short, including perhaps only one, two, or three "new" words. "The Cactus" is an example of a group-dictated story and the teacher-written account based on that story. The underlined words are "new" in that the children did not use those words in their story and have not (to the best of the teacher's knowledge) encountered those words in previous reading materials.

Dictated Story

THE CACTUS

The cactus feels prickly. When you go to the desert you can see lots of cactus. It grows where it's dry in the desert. The cactus keeps water inside to live on for a long time. Our cactus has a flower on it, but some of them don't have flowers. Our cactus has two yellow flowers.

Teacher-written Account

CACTUS

A desert is very dry because it does not get much <u>rain</u>. A cactus can grow in the desert because it does not need much water. Some kinds of cactus are very small and some grow very <u>large</u>. Many kinds of cactus have <u>needles</u> that feel prickly.

The teacher has chosen "new" words that are relatively uncomplicated phonetically and structurally so that phonetic and structural analysis can be applied successfully. Also the teacher has placed these "new" words in contexts that will aid the identification of those words. (For instance, the teacher recalled that the word *needles* was used in the preliminary discussion about the cactus. At that time the needles were described as prickly by the children. Thus, the teacher wrote of "needles that feel prickly," providing a better context clue for the identification of this word than a sentence such as *The cactus has needles*.

The teacher-prepared account can be used for a group lesson, the objective of which should be to use context, phonics, and structural analysis to analyze the "new" words. The teacher's story can be put on chart paper or duplicated so that each child has a copy. The teacher should have the children read the account silently first. Then different children can be asked to read portions of the account aloud. If there is hesitation at the "new" words, the teacher can lead the group through the steps of figuring out a new word (see page 52). Such a lesson may only require ten or fifteen minutes to complete and can give good practice in the exercise of word analysis skills. A number of such lessons should be planned over a period of weeks until the children display good abilities to analyze such "new" words.

Word Hunts

The teacher can have children look for unfamiliar words in published materials. A group can be gathered together and each child given different easy-to-read material. (Preprimers from a number of different series can be used.) When one child finds an unfamiliar word, the teacher can put the sentence containing the word on the chalkboard, and the group can work together to figure out the word. The child who has found the word can also be asked to show the group the relevant page in the book so that picture clues can be used as well. Not every child needs to find a "new" word. If the group analyzes three or four different words, the activity will have been worthwhile.

Teacher-written materials and word hunts can be introduced frequently, a few times a week, until the children have gained confidence and competence in analyzing many unfamiliar words. Usually a few weeks of such work will be adequate preparation for meeting the word-recognition demands of the "new" words in a basal series. However, some children will need more time to exercise these skills. Careful teacher observation is needed to assess progress, and the suggested activities should be continued until the children are able to identify most of the unfamiliar words that are introduced in these ways.

USING INFORMAL ASSESSMENTS OF PROGRESS

A few weeks or a month of transition-stage activities will provide most children with adequate preparation for moving into first-grade level materials. More time can be allowed for this stage, however, if children seem to need additional practice in analyzing unfamiliar words or wider exposure to easy-to-read materials. The teacher will need to observe children carefully in order to decide when to introduce group instruction in the primer or first reader. A number of informal evaluation procedures can be used during this time to determine strengths and weaknesses and to judge when children will be able to profit from regular basal instruction.

Informal Word-Recognition Test

An informal word-recognition test can be constructed to estimate a child's ability to handle the word-recognition demands of the primer or first reader planned for use in the classroom.

Constructing the test

1. Turn to the back of the book to the list of "new" words given for the book.
2. Count the total number of words in the list, excluding proper nouns.
3. Divide this total by 25.
4. Consider the answer obtained in Step 3 to be the Nth word. For instance, if there are 250 words on the list, the Nth word will be the tenth word (250 divided by 25 = 10).
5. Starting with the first word on the list, include every Nth word on the test list, again excluding proper nouns.
6. The end result will be a test list of 25 words that have been chosen randomly from the total list.
7. If the book does not have a word list at the end, construct the test as follows to allow for a random sample of words.
    a. Divide the total number of pages by 25.
    b. On each Nth page take the fifth (or seventh or tenth) word to include on the list.
    c. Exclude proper nouns or words that have already been included from a previous page.

Administering the test

1. Give one child a copy of the word list. Make sure the words are clearly typed and well spaced (see Appendix F).
2. Have a record sheet to mark the child's responses (see Appendix F).
3. Tell the child to read down the list. (Assure children that they are not expected to know all the words.)
4. As the child reads, put a check mark by those words recognized immediately, i.e., with no more than two or three seconds' hesitation.
    a. If a child hesitates longer than three seconds, just say, "Skip that word and try the next one."
    b. If a child miscalls a word, write down what is said but do not ask for a correction of the error.
5. Continue until the child has tried each word on the list.
6. After the child has completed the list, have him take another

look at any missed words to see how word analysis skills are applied. *Give no help*; see what the child can do independently.

7. As testing proceeds, do not tell the child a response is right or wrong. Always give assurances that the performance is "very good" or "fine" without giving specific comments as to the accuracy.

Interpreting results. Count the number of checks, i.e., those words identified immediately, and compute the percentage of correct immediate responses. This figure will provide an estimate of the child's sight vocabulary as it relates to the book from which the test was constructed.

We have found that scores of 50%–60% suggest that children have a large enough sight vocabulary to be instructed in a first reader. This percentage is lower than the usual criterion for instructional level, but in practice it seems to be adequate for success in the book. Scores of less than 50% in most instances suggest that the child will have difficulty with the book in question.

An informal word-recognition test provides only an estimate of the child's ability to handle a particular book comfortably. Scores on this test should be interpreted in light of the child's overall progress in developing reading skills and should never be used as the sole criterion for deciding when a child is able to work successfully in the chosen first reader.

Oral Reading Assessment

Regular informal assessment of oral reading skills can also be made at this time, since children will continue to read dictated stories and will read aloud portions of easy-to-read materials in sharing sessions with one or more children. The teacher may also ask individual children to read aloud selected portions of various materials specifically for the purpose of assessing fluency and accuracy of oral reading. Assessment of oral reading skills can be used along with other information, e.g., performance on an informal word-recognition test, to determine if the child seems ready for group instruction in a particular basal reader.

Most reading experts have long used specific quantitative criteria for assessing oral reading skills, based on the percentage of correctly identified words in a given passage. The assumption has been that children should miscall no more than five out of one hundred consecutive words in order for their performance to be considered adequate for successful work in the materials at hand. Thus the following criteria are usually used:

Below 95%   Frustration level
95%   Instructional level
99%   Independent level

Recent research and theories in the field, however, have called these criteria into question.* It has been recognized that some errors are more significant than others and thus that all errors should not be given equal weight in assessing performance. Also, it is recognized that most children in the beginning stages of reading can often miscall more words than five out of one hundred and yet comprehend the material quite well. Thus, we recommend that consideration be given to the qualitative aspects of the child's oral reading at this stage rather than the quantitative. That is, the teacher may use the percentage of accuracy in oral reading as a part of the evaluation of a child's skills but should probably place more emphasis on the quality of the child's reading and the overall approach to the task of oral reading. If a child meets most or all of the following qualitative criteria when reading aloud, the performance should be judged satisfactory:

1. The oral reading is generally fluent rather than hesitant or word by word.
2. The oral reading shows reasonable attention to appropriate intonation and expression.
3. Errors in word recognition generally do not change the meaning of the sentence or passage. For example, substituting *a* for *the* or *puppy* for *dog* would almost never significantly change the meaning of a selection and thus should be considered insignificant deviations from the text.
4. Errors in word recognition that are semantically or syntactically inappropriate are usually noticed and corrected by the child.
5. The child attempts to figure out unknown words encountered in a reading passage and is successful on some occasions.

*William Powell, "The Validity of the Instructional Reading Level," in R. E. Leibert, ed., *Diagnostic Viewpoints in Reading* (Newark, Delaware: International Reading Association, 1971).

Kenneth Goodman, "A Psycholinguistic Guessing Game," in H. Singer and R. Ruddell, eds., *Theoretical Models and Processes of Reading* (Newark, Delaware: International Reading Association, 1970).

These informal measures (a word-recognition test and an oral reading assessment) can be formalized to provide a relatively objective measure of progress. Appendix F contains complete directions for constructing and using a set of informal measures that we have used successfully to judge whether children are ready to move into a regular basal reader book.

PROVIDING FOR INDIVIDUAL DIFFERENCES: CHILDREN WHO MAKE SLOWER PROGRESS

Most chidlren in a typical first-grade class will make good progress in a language-experience program. The average child will begin acquiring a sight vocabulary the first week of school and, after four or five months of participation in the program, will be ready or almost ready to handle a primer or first reader. However, some will make slower progress, collecting perhaps only ten to twenty words in their word banks at the end of the same four or five months of work. The teacher may be tempted to think that there is something "wrong" with these individuals, especially if there are many others in the class who are learning at a much more rapid rate. The teacher may also think the program itself is inappropriate for those pupils who do not learn as quickly as others.

Since the language-experience approach is such a highly individualized program, it should be recognized that wide differences in achievement levels will occur simply because of the wide variation among the children in the class. Children differ greatly intellectually, socially, emotionally, and physically; differences in reading achievement are reflections of these other differences and should be expected and accepted. In fact, wide individual differences are recognized more quickly and easily in a language-experience program than in a typical basal approach to beginning reading. This is because language-experience procedures are not aimed at the "average" child, as are the usual basal reader programs. In a language-experience program all children can learn as many words and skills as they are able to master and can accomplish these learnings at their own rates. No child is restricted by beginning reading materials of strictly graded, highly limited content and language. Thus, some very able children will make extremely rapid progress, and the differences between these children and the less achieving pupils will be accordingly widened.

With the children who make slower progress, it is more reasonable to accept their differences, learn to recognize their needs, and adjust lessons and activities accordingly, rather than to assume there is something "wrong" with the children or the program.

Children who are having difficulty will display some or all of the following characteristics:

1. Difficulty learning sight words
2. Frequent forgetting of previously learned sight words
3. Difficulty rereading previously dictated stories
4. Shorter attention span for independent and teacher-directed activities
5. Greater attentiveness to the stimulus and discussion than to the recording and reading of the experience story
6. Relatively poorly developed handwriting skills
7. Difficulty with beginning word-attack skills and activities

When it becomes clear that some children are having difficulty, modifications in their programs are needed to match their rates of learning, meet their individual needs, and prevent the frustration and restlessness that can result from the difficulties they have. There are many reasons that children have trouble mastering basic reading skills; any adjustments should reflect an accurate assessment of the source of the difficulty. We cannot anticipate and list every source of difficulty children may have, but we do recognize that some children have short attention spans, display relatively immature behavior and attitudes in relation to their peers, or have particular difficulty retaining words and mastering basic word-attack skills. When any or all of the characteristics listed above become evident, one or more of the following modifications is advisable:

1. *Limit the duration of any single lesson or independent activity.* Instead of working with these children for a single, thirty-minute stretch, plan three ten-minute or two fifteen-minute lessons to accomplish the same goals. In the intervals between lessons, plan other short and varied activities in line with their interests and needs. For instance, part of a morning schedule for such children might be like the following:

9:00– 9:15	Observe and discuss stimulus for dictation
9:15– 9:30	Work on jigsaw puzzles, drawing, and other active, nonreading tasks
9:30– 9:40	Dictate story about stimulus; reread once or twice
9:40– 9:45	Draw picture to go with story
9:45–10:00	Class recess
10:00–10:10	Reread dictation with teacher supervision

2. *Limit the length of any single dictated story*. Some children find experience stories of average length (25–40 words) too frustrating to handle. Stories with only one or two sentences (15–20 words) can be easier to deal with.
3. *Provide many extra opportunities for repetition and reinforcement of skills*. For instance:
   a. Have the children read the dictated story with teacher help more times than the usual procedures suggest.
   b. Plan frequent review sessions to reread previously dictated stories and go over word cards.
   c. Record one or two familiar dictated stories on tape; have the children listen to the tape while following along in the story book.
4. *Give individual attention*. Provide opportunities for the child to work individually with a more able reader (a peer, an older child, a teacher's aide). Word games, rereading of dictated stories, or word-bank activities can be assigned.

SUMMARY

The success of the language-experience approach depends as much on a well-planned continuing program as on initial success with word banks and dictated stories. The overall goals are maintaining interest in reading, developing habits of wide reading, and increasing reading skills. These will be accomplished with a well-maintained and well-used classroom library, successful transition to a formal basal program, intelligent use of informal diagnostic procedures, and attention to individual differences.

Chapter VIII

Evaluation
of
Pupil Progress

Several approaches can be taken to evaluate student progress in a language-experience program. Standardized tests and informal measures can both be used to good advantage. But tests and other measures of student achievement should not be used without careful thought to

1. The basic objectives of the program
2. The appropriateness of the measurement technique
3. The utility of the evaluation procedure

In this chapter we will present some guidelines to evaluation with attention to these three important considerations.

EVALUATION BASED ON INSTRUCTIONAL OBJECTIVES

The following are the general objectives of a language-experience program:

1. To develop readers' sight vocabularies at each child's optimal rate of learning
2. To develop readers with flexible and effective word-attack skills
3. To develop basic word-meaning and comprehension skills at all stages

4. To maintain positive attitudes toward reading
5. To develop readers with habits of reading a wide variety of informative and entertaining books

Some measure of the success of meeting each of these objectives is needed for a balanced system of evaluation. That is, the success of an LEA program should not be judged on student performance in only one or two areas. We will suggest some procedures for evaluating each of the five objectives listed, recognizing that other, comparable techniques might also be used.

Evaluation of Sight Vocabulary

The evaluation of sight vocabulary growth can best be accomplished through the frequent and periodic use of informal measures. A few suggestions follow.

1. *Periodic checks of retention of words in word banks.* Have individuals read off their word cards to check retention. In early weeks children can go through all their cards at one sitting; a weekly check will only take a few moments per child. As children acquire more words, plan several short checking sessions over a period of a week or ten days to allow for adequate assessment of all words. For instance, announce that all the *p, q, r, s,* and *t* words are to be checked on a particular day.

Children will not all learn the same number of words from week to week; they will show individual patterns in learning that will allow their performance to be judged in comparison with others in the class.

Remove forgotten words from the bank for relearning activities. (The "I forgot" envelope is useful at this time.) Keep records of the number of words known and of the proportion of forgotten words compared to known words so that patterns of learning can be described and comparisons among children can be made.

This procedure is most useful in the beginning stages of the program when word banks are being established and used daily. Word banks then reflect most of the sight vocabulary that is being acquired.

2. *Periodic informal word-recognition tests.* Use lists of words taken from basal reader books to assess progress in the acquisition of sight vocabulary. Many series provide such lists for their preprimer, primer, and first reader books; teacher-made lists can also be constructed from these materials. Make quick checks

whenever it would be useful to assess pupils' abilities to deal with these "basal words." (See pages 138–39 for explanation of this testing technique.)

This procedure will be most appropriate when children are in the transition stage. At this point the teacher may be considering some group instruction in some basal materials and want to know if the children are ready to deal with the demands of a particular book. Or, the teacher may simply want to make a quick comparison with where children might be expected to "be" in a given basal series.

3. *Informal observations of children's sight vocabulary strength.* Many opportunities exist daily to check sight vocabulary informally. As children read one another's stories, play word-card games, browse through library books, and complete other independent activities, they will be demonstrating their skills of learning and retaining sight vocabulary. Observations of behavior at these tasks will provide good subjective information on progress. Records do not need to be kept, but over time the cumulative effect of observations will be helpful in evaluating pupil progress.

Evaluation of Word-Attack Skills

Student progress in mastering several word-attack strategies needs to be evaluated regularly. Use of context clues, phonetic analysis, and structural analysis all should be assessed. Some standardized tests contain subtests that measure word-attack skills; such instruments can be used at the end of the school year as one mark of student progress. However, frequent informal assessment of growth in these skills is needed throughout the year. Whatever informal measures are used, the overall goal of establishing an effective and flexible word-attack strategy should not be forgotten. That is, children may differ in their abilities to use different specific word-attack skills, and it is not important that all children learn all skills equally well. What is important is that all children develop a workable system that enables them to identify most unknown words. With these ideas in mind, we offer a few suggestions for assessment in this area.

Use of Context Clues

1. During follow-up work with dictated stories, when children are unable to identify some words in isolation, ask them to reread the sentence from the story in which the unfamiliar word occurs.

(See page 18 for a step-by-step procedure to use.) Keep anecdotal records of performance to measure progress.

2. Construct sentences or short accounts using several known words (words from a group story that children have mastered) and several "new" words (words chosen because they are probably unfamiliar to the pupils). Ask children to read aloud these "test" sentences. Keep records of the number or percentage of "new" words correctly identified.

3. Construct simple exercises (using familiar words from dictated stories) that leave out some words that could be guessed by using context clues. After teaching children how to do such cloze exercises, use these periodically to check children's abilities to make intelligent guesses about what goes in the blanks. (Give credit for all meaningful and appropriate responses.) These exercises can be done orally or, when children are able to write easily, can be presented as written exercises. Keep records of children's scores on these informal "tests."

Use of phonetic and structural analysis. Since the goal of phonics/structural analysis instruction is to help children apply this knowledge to figure out unfamiliar words while reading, the best measure of progress in this area is, simply, to note how well children figure out "new" words in their ongoing reading of a variety of materials. Regular teacher observation of children's day-to-day performance will give the best evaluative information. However, several types of specific assessments of phonics/structure skills can be used to measure childrens' progress in applying these word attack strategies. We will suggest several procedures that can be used regularly for evaluation.

1. For children who are just beginning to learn the basics of phonics principles, auditory discrimination training is essential. (See pages 55–59.) At this early stage, informal assessments of auditory discrimination ability are valuable for marking progress in readiness to learn sound-letter associations. Give children periodic "tests" of auditory discrimination using lists of paired words, some of which begin (end) with the same sound and some of which begin (end) with a different sound. As consonant sounds are introduced, periodic assessment of auditory discrimination will be useful for determining mastery of this skill. Use lists of ten to fifteen paired words for group or individual assessment. Record performance to measure progress and to plan continuing instruction.

2. Exercises in consonant and vowel substitution can be used to

advantage to test pupils' abilities to apply phonetic analysis skills. Construct lists of items (some words and some nonwords) for such test exercises. For instance, place consonants in front of several common word elements (*all: ball, call, dall* . . . ; *ish: bish, cish, dish* . . .) for testing purposes. Put these lists on the chalkboard or give each child a copy. Ask children to read down the list; make notes of correct/incorrect responses. After several such exercises, patterns of learning will emerge. Information about needed further phonics instruction can be obtained, and marks of progress in such learning can be kept.

3. Nonsense words provide a good way to check children's ability to apply knowledge of certain phonic elements. Use a list of nonsense words such as *tet, wab, mot, rup,* and *lif* to check children's knowledge of various consonant and vowel combinations. Or use nonsense words as part of phonics lessons to test for understanding of phonics elements or generalizations that have been taught. Or prepare a list of nonsense words for individual children to read aloud. Such a procedure will yield good evaluative data and good specific information for planning further instruction.

4. Application of phonics skills can also be judged when a child meets an unknown word in a book. Give a pupil a new book to read silently in your company. Tell the child, "Stop reading when you come to a word you don't know." When this happens, ask, "What do you think the word is?" Of course, the child may well be able to take advantage of the context and make an accurate guess. This is an appropriate behavior; praise the child for success and then ask him or her to continue reading until encountering an unfamiliar word that cannot be identified by using context clues. Ask the child to sound this one out. The response at this point will provide some information about phonics skills. For instance, if the unfamiliar word is *truck* in the sentence *Jay sat on his toy truck*, the child's response will show what phonic elements he seems to know. A response of *tick* would suggest attention to beginning and ending sounds; *try* would indicate knowledge of the initial blend; *tuck* would suggest mastery of the appropriate vowel sound plus the final consonant digraph. If the child says *train*, it would suggest that he is using context clues and is also responding correctly to the initial blend. Several such find-an-unknown-word sessions will provide good evaluative and diagnostic information on developing phonics skills.

5. Comparable procedures can be used for assessing structural

analysis skills. For instance, present pairs of singular/plural words (*cup/cups*) for oral reading to see if children can distinguish differences. Prepare similar "tests" for distinguishing roots from roots plus inflectional endings (*look/looking; walk/walked*).

6. From the time children begin to do creative writing, their knowledge of letter-sound relationships can be evaluated. Children are encouraged to spell words according to the sounds they hear. Thus their writing provides a graphic picture of an emerging consciousness of sounds and of phonic generalizations. It is not unusual, for instance, to observe when children generalize that a word with a long vowel sound often has a final silent *e*. Children will often write a final *e* when they hear a long vowel, as when they write *dide* (for *died*) or *lade* (for *laid*). At regular intervals read children's writing for purposes of diagnosing phonics skill development.

Evaluation of Comprehension

The development of comprehension skills is an integral part of a language-experience program. Dictated stories are highly meaningful because they are directly tied to real, usually recent experiences. Comprehension is not formally "taught," since basic understanding of the materials can be assumed. However, from the start it is important for children to see all kinds of printed materials as attempts to communicate meaningfully. Evaluation of comprehension skills can use a variety of materials, including dictated stories. Here are a few suggestions that can be used as guidelines for developing several good techniques for testing comprehension.

1. *Teacher story*. Compose a story using the vocabulary from several previously dictated stories. At the end of the "new" story list several questions for children to answer. (See page 136 for an example of a teacher-written story.)
2. *Retelling stories*. Ask individual children to read a portion of a story in a trade book and then retell it in their own words. Use a few prompting or encouraging comments or questions if a child seems unsure of how to proceed.
3. *Modified informal reading inventory*. A modified informal reading inventory (IRI) can be prepared using the last preprimer or the primer. Ask the child to read the first page of the story aloud and then retell it. The next page can be read silently and also retold. Ask some questions to see if children can recall informa-

tion they omitted in their retelling. (See Appendix F for an example of a modified informal reading inventory.)

4. *Standardized tests.* Some of the subtests of standardized reading tests are designed to measure comprehension. Observe performance on these measures to judge comprehension abilities. Judge such test scores in the context of the child's overall performance on informal, day-to-day measures of comprehension skills.

Informal evaluation of comprehension skills can occur in many regular classroom activities as well. For instance, teachers can observe children's abilities to read written directions on the chalkboard, labels on pictures, peers' word card sentences, or teacher-composed chart stories. There are many such possible measures of basic comprehension skills that should be used regularly to evaluate student progress in this area.

Evaluation of Attitudes

A very important goal of any reading program is the development and maintenance of positive attitudes toward reading and books. Children's first experiences with reading, especially, should leave them with the feeling that reading is pleasant, highly meaningful, and often exciting or informative. A successful beginning reading program is one that results in positive attitudes toward reading as well as acceptable levels of achievement. Here are some suggestions for evaluating pupil attitudes toward the program.

1. *Parent conferences.* Parent conferences can provide opportunities to check on children's attitudes toward reading. When meeting with parents, ask, "What does your youngster say about reading?" "Is he excited about reading?" "Does he talk about reading activities?" "Does he seek out books to read?" Parents will be able to provide good information about children's perceptions of the reading program. Note their comments in the child's folder and discuss any changes in attitude at the next conference.

2. *Teacher observation.* Note how children react when a reading task is suggested in school. Are there groans and delaying responses or do children respond in a positive manner? Watch for unpopular activities and judge whether or not negative responses are characteristic of the children's overall response. Also, observe attention span for various reading activities. Children who feel successful and happy about reading will be able to spend longer and longer times on various reading tasks.

3. *Free-time choices*. During play time or before and after school allow children to choose among a number of classroom activities. Watch what they choose. If children frequently "play school" using dictated chart stories, it is fair to assume that they enjoy reading stories. If instead of trucks, blocks, and puzzles children choose to play reading games, go through their word banks, or look at and read story books, they probably do so because they consider these activities fun.

Evaluation of children's attitudes toward reading is usually informal but nevertheless an important aspect of the overall plan for evaluation.

Evaluation of Habits of Wide Reading

One measure of the success of reading instruction is the number of books a child reads independently. In a language-experience classroom where teacher-directed activities are derived primarily from story charts, it is very important for children to have many opportunities for independent reading in trade books. Habits of wide reading can be encouraged by providing a varied book collection in the classroom. If one of the "high-priority" activities is reading books, teachers should see an increase in the number of books read as children's reading abilities increase. Number of books read can be tallied on a monthly basis. By mid-year, when most children's writing skills permit copying the book title, children can be encouraged to keep their own book records. Examination of this record will reveal not only the number of books read but also the breadth of topic selection.

CHOICE OF APPROPRIATE MEASUREMENT TECHNIQUES

Most of the measures we have suggested in this chapter are informal teacher-constructed tests or specific teacher observations. We have emphasized measures of this kind because they are probably the most appropriate evaluation procedures to use in a program that relies heavily on teacher-designed lessons and activities. Thoughtfully constructed, objectives-based teacher tests usually provide more valid measures of student progress in an LEA program than commercially published book tests or skill tests. For instance, a teacher might introduce the beginning consonant sounds of *b*, *n*, *t*, and *s* to an LEA group whose last two dictated stories contained many words with these beginning sounds. In this instance the most appropriate measure of student learning would be a teacher-made test (or tests) of these four sound-letter associations. The teacher might ask individuals to read *bike, nike, tike,* and *sike,* starting with a known key word such as *like* (or *bell, nell, tell* and *sell* starting with a known key word such as *well*), or might devise a written response sheet with pictures of *b, n, t,* and *s* words to match with the appropriate letters. These or other comparable procedures will provide a direct measure of student progress. It would be inappropriate to use a commercially developed phonics test at this point that would test knowledge of other sound-letter associations that might yet not have been introduced. Since teachers in LEA classrooms plan sequences of skill instruction according to what occurs in dictated stories and what children need, evaluation procedures should be devised to reflect the unique program than results from this approach.

Of course, not all evaluative instruments need be teacher-designed to be effective. Some commercially available materials can be profitably used at different points. For instance, some workbook pages or skill sheets may provide just the right exercises to test for mastery of different skill objectives. These measures should be sought out and used when they seem appropriate. Also, some commercial tests that accompany basal series or that are independent from any particular series may be used to advantage at different points throughout the year. For instance, informal reading inventories accompanying the first reader into which children are to be placed can be used to assess progress when children seem ready to move into that book. Or commercially prepared word-recognition lists from basal series or reading tests might be used as one way to assess achievement after children have well-established word banks.

Some measures are more appropriate at certain times in the school year than at other times. For instance, standardized reading tests, measuring very general reading objectives, are best used at the end of the school year, after the children have had adequate time to develop beginning reading skills. Book tests from basal series and other commercially prepared skill tests also probably provide more valid measures of progress after children have had reasonable exposure to books from a basal series. Thus, teacher-made, informal checks of progress are more valuable and effective at the start of the program, and commercially prepared materials are more appropriate nearer the end of the year.

Many decisions need to be made throughout the year concerning the types of tests to be used and the timing of test administration. We have suggested a few guidelines for devising appropriate evaluation procedures, recognizing that each evaluation program will differ depending on the resources and personnel available in a given school.

UTILITY OF THE EVALUATION PROCEDURE

Some reading programs spend considerable time testing children—to move pupils from one level to another, to assess progress with a myriad of skills, or to provide data for judging the success of the program in general. When a great deal of time is spent testing, i.e., with formal measures from reading tests or reading series, the amount of lost instructional time is certainly unfortunate, and the usefulness of the test results is often questionable. (How many tests do you need to make intelligent decisions?) Our suggestions here for evaluation procedures are made with this issue of utility in mind.

Valuable observations of student progress can be made through use of some of the informal measures we have suggested. Most such measures can serve a dual purpose—to provide basic evaluative data and to provide useful diagnostic information for planning further instruction. When evaluation becomes an integral part of daily classroom activities, i.e., when diagnostic teaching is used skillfully, separate testing times are not needed for evaluating student progress, and the program of evaluation will be efficient and useful. Knowledgeable, observant teachers who keep good records of many informal observations will have a wealth of material for evaluating the effectiveness of the program. Coupled with some intelligent use of standardized tests these informal procedures will provide a good program of evaluation.

SUMMARY

The success of a language-experience program, like any other reading program, can be judged best by seeing how much and how well children read stories and books and whether they exhibit positive attitudes while doing so. Specific reading skills, such as thorough knowledge of phonics, highly accurate oral reading, or well-developed sight vocabularies should not become the main focus of the program. Evaluation procedures should provide continual information on developing attitudes as well as specific skill development. Informal, teacher-made tests and some standardized or commercially prepared tests can be used for this purpose. The program of evaluation should be efficient and useful, aimed at measuring the success with which children are developing lifetime habits of enjoyable and informative reading.

APPENDICES

RECOMMENDED READINGS

INDEX

Appendix A

Directions for Book Binding

Materials:

    Heavy cardboard or covers from old books
    White construction paper or typing paper
    Large tapestry needle
    Heavy-duty thread
    Wallpaper, contact paper, or shelf paper (for cover)
    Rubber cement
    Colored construction paper (slightly smaller than cardboard covers)
    Colored tape 1½" wide

Procedures:

1. Fold sheets of either construction paper or typing paper in half to form pages of book. Trim to ½" smaller than cardboard cover.
2. Sew sheets of paper together along fold as shown, using a back stitch.

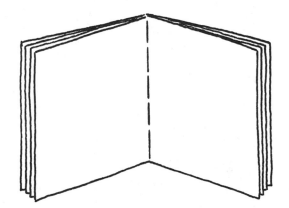

3. Cement cardboard to plain side of cover paper (wallpaper, contact paper, etc.) as shown, allowing ½″ between pieces and a 1″ border around the edge.

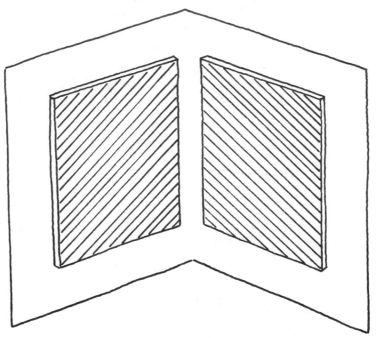

4. Cut out corners of cover paper. Fold in edges and cement them to cardboard. It might be better to fold top and bottom edges first, and side edges last, rather than folding in the sequence illustrated.

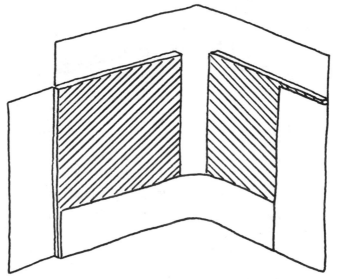

5. Position sewn book pages so that the fold is between the card-board pieces. Use colored tape to attach the first page, at the folded edge, to inside front cover as shown. Tape the last pages to inside back cover in the same way.

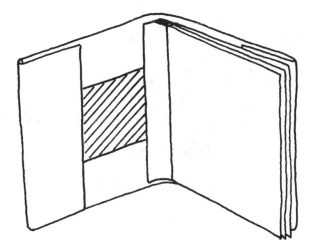

6. Cement colored construction paper to inside front and back covers to finish inside covers.
7. Reinforce outside spine of book with colored tape.

Dictated Story and Lists Generated for Remedial Instruction

A STAR IN THE SEA

A star in the sea is very funny. It is a starfish. This starfish is not a fish. It is a squid. It has cups that grab oysters. He has five legs usually. On every leg there is a lot of cups. When he grabs an oyster he pulls it apart with his cups. And if one leg gets tired he just lets it go and puts another leg in. The oyster fights the pull but he finally gives up. And the starfish eats him all up.

December 2

SEQUENTIAL LIST

A	not	five	an	he	but
star	a	legs	oyster	just	he
in	fish	usually	he	lets	finally
the	It	On	pulls	it	gives
sea	is	every	it	go	up
is	a	leg	apart	and	And
very	squid	there	with	puts	the
funny	It	is	his	another	starfish
It	has	a	cups	leg	eats
is	cups	lot	And	in	him
a	that	of	if	The	all
starfish	grab	cups	one	oyster	up
This	oysters	When	leg	fights	
starfish	He	he	gets	the	
is	has	grabs	tired	pull	

SCRAMBLE I

up	go	every
all	it	on
him	lets	legs
eats	just	five
starfish	tired	has
the	gets	that
and	one	squid
gives	apart	fish
he	pulls	not
but	an	this
pull	grabs	funny
fights	when	sea
oyster	of	star
in	lot	if
leg	a	cups
another	is	his
puts	there	with

SCRAMBLE II

star	that	up
sea	has	all
funny	legs	him
on	five	apart
is	an	cups
a	pulls	one
lot	his	if
of	gets	
lets	tired	
it	in	
go	oyster	
puts	fights	
leg	but	
this	be	
not	and	
fish	the	
squid	starfish	

Appendix C

Easy-to-Read Books

Here are some examples of easy-to-read books which can provide transition from language-experience to instruction in a basal reader.

Alexander, M. *Maybe a Monster*. New York: Dial Press, 1968.
———. *Blackboard Bear*. New York: Dial Press, 1969.
Anglund, J. W. *Cowboy's Secret Life*. New York: Harcourt, Brace & World, 1963.
Asheron, S. *Fraidy Cat*. New York: Grosset & Dunlap, 1970.
Attenberger, W. *Who Knows the Little Man?* New York: Random House, 1972.
Balian, L. *I Love You, Mary Jane*. New York: Abingdon, 1967.
———. *Where in the World Is Henry?* New York: Bradbury, 1972.
Barton, B. *Where's Al?* Somers, Conn.: Seabury Press, 1972.
Bel Geddes, B. *I Like to Be Me*. New York: The Viking Press, 1963.
Bonsall, C. *The Day I Had to Play with My Sister*. New York: Harper & Row, 1972.
Bright, R. *I Like Red*. Garden City, N.Y.: Doubleday, 1955.
Buckley, H. *Grandfather and I*. New York: Lathrop, 1959.
———. *Grandmother and I*. New York: Lathrop, 1961.
Budney, B. *A Kiss Is Round*. New York: Lathrop, 1954.
Burningham, J. *The Baby*. New York: Crowell, 1975.
Carle, E. *Have You Seen My Cat?* New York: Franklin Watts, 1973.
Carley, W. *Percy the Parrot Yelled Quiet*. Champaign, Ill.: Garrard, 1971.
Carroll, R. *Where's the Bunny?* New York: Oxford, 1950.
Darby, G. *Becky, the Rabbit*. Chicago: Benefic Press, 1964.
DeCaprio, A. *A Happy Day*. New York: Grosset & Dunlap, 1965.
DeLage, I. *Good Morning*. Champaign, Ill.: Garrard, 1974.
———. *Hello, Come In*. Champaign, Ill.: Garrard, 1971.
DePaola, T. *Andy, That's My Name*. Englewood Cliffs, N.J.: Prentice-Hall, 1973.

DeRegiers, B. *Catch a Little Fox*. Somers, Conn.: Seabury Press, 1970.

Derman, S. *Monkey Island*. Chicago: Benefic Press, 1957.

Domanska, J. *If All the Seas Were One Sea*. New York: Macmillan, 1971.

Eggleston, J. *Things That Grow*. Chicago: Melmont, 1958.

Emberley, E. *Green Says Go*. Boston: Little, Brown, 1968.

Furamata, E. *How Not to Catch A Mouse*. New York: Oxford, 1950.

Grossbart, F. *A Big City*. New York: Harper & Row, 1966.

Hoff, S. *Who Will Be My Friends?* New York: Harper & Row, 1960.

Howard, C. *Let's Go Shopping*. New York: Grosset & Dunlap, 1975.

———. *Mom and Me*. New York: Grosset & Dunlap, 1975.

Lapshire, R. *Put Me in The Zoo*. New York: Random House, 1960.

Latham, J. *Who Lives Here?* Champaign, Ill.: Garrand, 1974.

LeSieg, T. *The Eye Book*. New York: Random House, 1968.

———. *Ten Apples up on Top*. New York: Random House, 1966.

Lewi, B. *We Like Noise*. Champaign, Ill.: Garrard, 1974.

McClintock, M. *What Have I Got?* New York: Harper & Row, 1961.

McGovern, A. *Too Much Noise*. Boston: Houghton Mifflin, 1967.

McInnes, J. *How Pedro Got His Name*. Champaign, Ill.: Garrard, 1974.

Myller, L. *No, No*. New York: Simon & Schuster, 1971.

Nodest, J. *Go Away Dog*. New York: Harper & Row, 1965.

Paulet, V. *Blue Bug and the Bullies*. Chicago: Children's Press, 1971.

———. *Blue Bug's Safety Book* Chicago: Children's Press, 1973.

Peppe, R. *The Alphabet Book*. New York: Four Winds Press, 1968.

Perkins, *A Hand Hand, Fingers, Thumb*. New York: Random House, 1969.

———. *The Ear Book*. New York: Random House, 1968.

Rand, A. & P. *I Know a Lot of Things*. New York: Harcourt, Brace & World, 1956.

Reit, S. *Round Things Everywhere*. New York: McGraw-Hill, 1969.

Seuss, Dr. *Fox in Socks*. New York: Random House, 1965.

———. *Hop on Pop*. New York: Random House, 1963.

———. *Green Eggs and Ham*. New York: Random House, 1960.

———. *One Fish, Two Fish, Red Fish, Blue Fish*. New York: Random House, 1960.

Shaw, C. *It Looked Like Spilt Milk*. New York: Harper & Row, 1947.

Slobodkin, L. *One Is Good but Two Is Better*. New York: Vanguard, 1956.

———. *Up High and Down Low*. New York: Macmillan, 1960.

Spier, P. *Crash, Bang, Boom*. New York: Doubleday, 1972.

Sullivan, J. *Round Is a Pancake*. New York: Holt, Rinehart & Winston, 1963.

Teague, K. *What Happened to Hector?* Champaign, Ill.: Garrard, 1974.

Tensen, R. *Come to the Pet Shop*. Chicago: Reilly & Lee, 1954.

——. *Come to the Zoo*. Chicago: Reilly & Lee, 1948.

Wellesley, H. *All Kinds of Neighbors*. New York: Holt, Rinehart & Winston, 1963.

Williams, G. *The Chicken Book*. New York: Delacorte, 1970.

Zolotow, C. *Some Things Go Together*. New York: Abelard-Schuman, 1969.

——. *Big Brother*. New York: Harper & Row, 1960.

Easy-to-Read Series

Here is a list of publishers' series of easy-to-read books that contain titles suitable for transition from language-experience stories to reading books.

Benefic Press:
    Animal Adventures

Thomas Crowell:
    Let's Read and Find Out Science Books

Garrard Publishing Co.:
    Venture Books

Golden Press (Western Publishing Co.):
    Golden Beginning Readers

Grosset and Dunlap (Wonder Books):
    Easy Readers

Harper and Row:
    Early I Can Read Books
    I Can Read Books

Holt, Rinehart and Winston:
    Bill Martin's Instant Readers

Macmillan:
    Ready to Read Books

Random House:
    Bright and Early Books
    Early Bird Books
    Beginner Books

Picture Books without Words

Alexander, M. *Out! Out! Out!*. New York: Dial Press, 1968.

———. *Bobo's Dream*. New York: Dial Press, 1970.

Amoss, B. *By the Sea*. New York: Parents' Magazine Press, 1969.

Anno, M. *Topsy-Turvies*. New York: Walker/Weatherbill, 1970.

Carroll, R. *Rolling Downhill*. New York: Henry Walck, 1973.

———. *What Whiskers Did*. New York: Henry Walck, 1965.

Degen, B. *Aunt Possum and the Pumpkin Man*. New York: Harper & Row, 1977.

DeGroat, D. *Alligator's Toothache*. New York: Crown, 1977.

Gilbert, E. *A Cat Story*. New York: Holt, Rinehart & Winston, 1963.

Goodall, J. *Creepy Castle*. New York: Atheneum, 1975.

———. *The Adventures of Paddy Pork*. New York: Harcourt, Brace & World, 1968.

Goshorn, E. *Shoestrings*. Minneapolis: Carol Rhoda, 1975.

Hutchins, P. *Changes, Changes*. New York: Macmillan, 1971.

Krahn, F. *Who's Seen the Scissors?* New York: Dutton, 1975.

———. *Sebastian and the Mushroom*. New York: Dutton, 1976.

———. *Catch That Cat*. New York: Dutton, 1978.

Mari, I. & E. *The Chicken and the Egg*. New York: Pantheon, 1969.

Mayer, M. *Bubble Bubble*. New York: Parents' Magazine Press, 1973.

Olschewski, A. *Winterbird*. Boston: Houghton Mifflin, 1969.

Simmons, E. *Dog*. New York: David McKay, 1967.

Ward, L. *The Silver Pony*. Boston: Houghton Mifflin, 1973.

Appendix F

Modified Informal Reading Inventory

Following are directions for constructing and using a set of informal measures for judging readiness for a basal primer or first reader.

The examples presented here are based on *A Place for Me* (Level 7: primer) and *Can You Imagine* (Level 6: the last pre-primer) of the Holt Basic Reading System (Holt, Rinehart & Winston, 1973). The same procedures can be used to construct and use similar informal tests to accompany any basal reader program.

Informal Word-Recognition Test
Construct an informal word-recognition test, as described on page 138 of this book, from the primer or first reader of the series, i.e., the book into which the children will move. (See p. 168 for an example.)

Oral and Silent Reading Selections
Use the first two or three pages of the last story in the last preprimer of the series for the oral reading selection. Use the next two or three pages as a silent reading selection. For the silent reading selection, compose three questions—one factual question and two for which answers require inferences to be made. (See p. 169 for examples of oral and silent reading selections.)

Administering and Interpreting Results

1. Administer the word-recognition test.
2. Give the child a copy of the oral reading selection as it appears in the preprimer; either use a copy of the book or a copy of the pages on which the selection appears. Ask the pupil to predict what might happen in the story to focus attention on the material and set a purpose for reading.

3. While the child reads aloud, mark a copy of the selection, indicating errors the child makes. The following errors should be marked:
   a. Words for which teacher help is required, i.e., words the child obviously does not know and that are supplied by the teacher.
   b. Words that are miscalled, e.g., *house* for *horse*, *dog* for *pet*, etc. (Even if the miscalled word is a meaningful deviation from the text, for testing purposes it is counted as an error.)
   c. Words that are omitted.

   Words that are miscalled and spontaneously corrected by the reader are not counted as errors.
4. Tell the child to continue reading the rest of the selection silently. Remind the reader to read carefully because questions will be asked following the reading.
5. When the child has finished reading silently, ask the three questions that have been made up to go with that part of the selection.

For useful record keeping of these informal assessments, a summary record sheet can be used. (On p. 170 there is an example of a record sheet that accompanies the word-recognition test and oral/silent reading assessment illustrated here.)

The examples shown here have been used with many children. We have found that children who score 7 or more are ready for group instruction in the book from which the word-recognition test was made. We emphasize, however, that these are informal measures. Our criterion of 7 may not be suitable for use in all classrooms with all kinds of materials. We urge teachers to try the procedure we describe and make their own judgments about an appropriate cut-off score based on what they observe in their own classrooms.

WORD RECOGNITION TEST: PRIMER

1. sick	10. then	19. afternoon
2. but	11. liked	20. home
3. came	12. noise	21. bench
4. carnival	13. daddy	22. trees
5. morning	14. sleeps	23. have
6. wanted	15. small	24. animals
7. I'm	16. Bob	25. streets
8. can't	17. played	
9. stopped	18. park	

ORAL AND SILENT READING SELECTIONS: PREPRIMER*

THE BIG CITY

(Oral Reading)

A burro went down a country road. She saw a frog in the road.

"Little frog," said the burro. "I want to go to the city. I want to see people and stores and cars and big houses. Where is the city?"

"Here is a sign," said the frog. "It tells where to go. Can you read it?" "No!" said the burro.

(Silent Reading)

"I will read the sign for you," said the frog. "It says, 'To the City.' Go down the road, and you will find the city."

The burro went down the road. She saw a sign. And she saw three sheep.

"Who can read the sign?" asked the burro. "I want to find the city."

"I can read the sign," said the big sheep. "It says, 'To the City.' Go down the road and you will find the city."

SUMMARY SHEET: INFORMAL ASSESSMENTS

Name _____

Total (12) _____

1. Word-recognition test (*A Place for Me*)   (3)_____
        60% or better ____ excellent ____ 3
        50% to 59% _____ good _____ 2
        40% to 49% _____ poor _____ 1
        0% to 39% _____ 0

2. Oral reading (*Can You Imagine*, pp. 53–54)   (3)_____
        0 to 1 error ____ excellent ____ 3
        2 to 3 errors ____ good _____ 2
        4 to 5 errors _____ poor _____ 1
        6 or more errors _____ 0

3. Retelling (*Can You Imagine*, pp. 53–54)   (3)_____
        excellent _____ 3
        good _____ 2
        poor _____ 1
        failure _____ 1

4. Silent reading (*Can You Imagine*, pp. 55–57)
   Questions:
        a. What did the Frog say the sign said?   (1)_____
             (to the city)
        b. How do you know the burro didn't know how   (1)_____
             to find the city? (he asked who could read
             the sign and said he wanted to find the city)
        c. How do you know the sheep couldn't read well?   (1) _____
             (sign said "beans," he said it was "to the city")

Recommended Readings

Ashland, Linda. "Conducting Individual Language Experience Stories." *Reading Teacher* 27 (November 1973):167–170.

Berko, Jean. "The Child's Language and Written Language." *Education* 85 (November 1965):151–153.

Cramer, Ronald. "Dialectology— A Case for Language Experience." *Reading Teacher* 25 (October 1971):32–39.

————. "Diagnosing Skills by Analyzing Children's Writing." *Reading Teacher* 30 (December 1976):276–279.

Dinan, Linda. "By the Time I'm Ten I'll Probably Be Famous." *Language Arts* 54 (October 1977):750–755.

Dixon, Carol. "Language Experience Stories as a Diagnostic Tool." *Language Arts* 54 (May 1977):501–505.

————. "Teaching Strategies for the Mexican-American Child." *Reading Teacher* 30 (November 1976):141–145.

Feely, Joan. "A Workshop Tried and True: Language Experience for Bilinguals." *Reading Teacher* 33 (October 1979):25–27.

Garman, Dorothy. "Language Patterns and Beginning Readers." *Reading Teacher* 31 (January 1978):393–396.

Goodman, Kenneth. "Reading: The Key Is in Children's Language." *Reading Teacher* 25 (March 1972):505–508.

Graves, Donald. "A Six-Year-Old's Writing Process: The First Half of First Grade." *Language Arts* 56 (October 1979):829–835.

Hall, Maryanne. "Linguistically Speaking Why Language Experience?" *Reading Teacher* 25 (January 1972):329–331.

Henderson, Edmund. "Group Instruction in a Language-Experience Approach." *Reading Teacher* 26 (March 1973):589–597.

Johnson, Terry. "Language Experience: We Can't All Write What We Can Say." *Reading Teacher* 31 (December 1977):297–299.

Kavale, Kenneth, and Schreiner, Robert. "Psycholinguistic Implications for Beginning Reading Instruction." *Language Arts* 55 (January 1978):34–40.

Lefevre, Carl. "Simplistic Standard Word-Perception Theory of Reading." *Elementary English* 45 (March 1968):349–353, 355.

Maya, Antonia. "Write to Read: Improving Reading Through Creative Writing." *Reading Teacher* 32 (April 1979):813–817.

Meltzer, Nancy, and Herse, Robert. "The Boundaries of Written Words as Seen by First Graders." *Journal of Reading Behavior* 1 (Summer 1969):3–14.

Quandt, Ivan. "Investing in Word Banks—A Practice for Any Approach." *Reading Teacher* 27 (November 1973):171–173.

Sorensen, Marilou, and Kerstetter, Kristen. "Phonetic Spelling: A Case Study." *Language Arts* 56 (October 1979):798–803.

Stauffer, Russell. "The Language Experience Approach to Reading Instruction for Deaf and Hearing Impaired Children." *Reading Teacher* 33 (October 1979):21–24.

Wiesendanger, K., and Birlem, E. "Adapting Language Experience to Reading for Bilingual Pupils." *Reading Teacher* 32 (March 1979):671–673.

Index